Leaders
of the
New School

Advancing Public Education from the Industrial Age to the Innovation Era

DR. DOUGLAS HENDRIX SR.

Copyright ©2024

INFINITY

DEDICATION

To my beautiful wife, Dr. Chato Hendrix, and our incredible children, Dove and Deuce.

Chato, you are the definition of grace and strength. Your tireless work as the Director of the Atlanta Falcons Cheerleaders, a career professional school counselor, a life coach, and a speaker reminds me daily of the incredible power of dedication and passion. You inspire not only me but everyone fortunate enough to witness your brilliance. Watching you balance your professional life while supporting your family is extraordinary. I am forever in awe of you.

To Dove and Deuce, my pride and joy, being your father, is my most incredible honor. I strive daily to make the world a better place for you, to guide you with love, and to show you through my work what it means to care for others honestly. You are my light, and everything I do is for you.

You are my heart and my most significant source of inspiration. Every day, when I see other children, I see your faces in theirs. I want for them what I wish for you—an unyielding sense of love, security, and the opportunities to chase every dream. This deep connection to our family is why I remain committed to every aspect of your life, giving all I can so that every step you take is toward greatness.

With all my love,

Douglas

"I am no longer accepting the things I cannot change. I am changing the things I cannot accept." ~ Angela Y. Davis

CONTENTS

FOREWORD

As Superintendent of Clayton County Public Schools, I am proud to witness firsthand the daily dedication and innovation our educators and leaders bring to this district. We are in a moment of tremendous opportunity, where reimagining education is no longer a luxury but a necessity. The education system must evolve in our increasingly complex world to meet future demands. This book, authored by Dr. Douglas Hendrix Sr., Senior Deputy Superintendent and Chief of Staff for Clayton County Public Schools, lays out a compelling vision for the future of education.

Dr. Hendrix's deep-rooted commitment to this district and his nearly 30 years of leadership in public education bring a unique and invaluable perspective to this work. His leadership has been instrumental in shaping the district's future, providing the strategic oversight necessary to lead one of Georgia's largest school systems with more than 51,000 students and 7,300 employees. His passion for innovative educational approaches is reflected throughout the ideas presented in this book, offering a pathway to transform how we think about teaching and learning.

The Master Teacher and Apprentice Model introduced here is particularly groundbreaking. It takes a bold step towards empowering educators as both teachers and leaders, fostering a collaborative and supportive environment where they can thrive. This approach helps address the critical issues of teacher shortages and enhances the quality of instruction for all students. The model reflects our shared goal at Clayton County Public Schools: to provide equitable, high-quality education that prepares every student for a rapidly changing world.

What makes this vision so compelling is its commitment to equity and innovation. Clayton County serves a diverse student population with unique challenges and needs. This book challenges us to rethink traditional methods and embrace technology, flexible learning environments, and real-world problem-solving to serve our students better. The emphasis on project-based learning and collaborative teaching practices aligns with our district's ongoing efforts to ensure that every child, regardless of background, has access to an excellent education.

As Dr. Hendrix outlines, change is difficult, but essential. This book provides a roadmap for reform and practical steps to realize this vision. It calls on all stakeholders—teachers, leaders, parents, and the broader community—to join forces in shaping a future where education serves as the foundation for success for individual students and society as a whole.

I have worked closely with Dr. Hendrix for years, and his vision is deeply rooted in a desire to see our students excel. His work is not just theoretical; it is a blueprint for how districts like ours can rise to the challenge of 21st-century education. I am confident that the ideas in this book will inspire educators and leaders everywhere to think differently and act boldly.

Let us embrace this opportunity to transform education and ensure we prepare our students for today, tomorrow, and beyond.

Dr. Anthony W. Smith

Superintendent, Clayton County Public Schools

PREFACE

Education has long been regarded as the foundation for future success for individuals and society. However, as I reflect on the journey we have taken as a nation and as global citizens, I cannot help but notice how the public school system, which once stood as a pillar of opportunity and progress, has not evolved at the same pace as the world. This book is a call to action—a vision for what education could be and what it should be for future generations.

As Senior Deputy Superintendent and Chief of Staff for Clayton County Public Schools, I have seen firsthand the triumphs and challenges that face our education system. I have also witnessed the passion and resilience of our educators, leaders, and students, who strive daily to make the most of what they are given. However, despite their efforts, I know that we can do better. We must do better. The future demands it.

The ideas presented in this book are rooted in a desire for radical transformation. We can no longer be satisfied with patchwork reforms and incremental changes. We must rethink every aspect of education—from governance and leadership to teaching models and classroom design. This is not about pointing fingers or dwelling on past failures. It is about seizing the opportunity to create a system that works for all students, no matter their background, zip code, or circumstances.

At the core of this vision is the belief that every child deserves the highest quality education possible. It is a system that values collaboration over competition, where Master Teachers lead the way in shaping instruction, and Apprentice Teachers learn from the best to ensure continuity of excellence. It is a system where governance is grounded in accountability and transparency, and where technology and innovation are embraced to enhance, not replace, the human element in education.

This book is for all stakeholders—teachers, parents, community leaders, and policymakers—because I believe everyone has a role to play in shaping the future of education. As you read through these chapters, I invite you to imagine a school system that is not just reformed but completely reimagined, a system where every decision is made with one question in mind: What about the children?

We stand at the crossroads of possibility and change. The time is now, the vision is clear, and the responsibility is ours.

Dr. Douglas Hendrix Sr.

Senior Deputy Superintendent - Chief of Staff, Clayton County Public Schools

INTRODUCTION
From One-Room Schoolhouses to the Future

Public education in America has come a long way from its colonial origins. Back then, informal learning was shaped by local religious leaders, primarily to ensure literacy for reading the Bible (Cubberley, 1920). Education was scarce and accessible only to a privileged few, typically in one-room schoolhouses. These schools, guided by minimally trained teachers, catered to students of all ages, aiming to equip them with basic literacy, writing, and arithmetic skills to function in society.

The need for a more organized education system became evident as the colonies gained independence. Reformers like Horace Mann played a pivotal role in this transformation, advocating for publicly funded education accessible to all children, regardless of wealth or social standing. Mann's vision of 'common schools,' where children from all backgrounds could learn together, was revolutionary. This early push laid the foundation for the formal public education system we recognize today, marking a significant step forward in the evolution of education (Mann, 1848). The progress from the one-room schoolhouses to the common schools, inspired by Mann's vision, gives us hope for further advancements in the future.

A significant turning point in the history of public education came in 1847 with the introduction of the Akron School Law in Ohio. This landmark legislation revolutionized education delivery by introducing the graded school system (Cubberley, 1920). For the first time, students were grouped by age, hoping that ability would accompany this new grouping, a far cry from the old one-room schoolhouses. For the time, this innovative approach laid the groundwork for the K-12 structure that we still use today, marking another crucial milestone in the evolution of education.

Despite these innovations, public education's core structure has remained unchanged since the 19th century. Students progress through grade levels is based on age, adhering to rigid curricula and prioritizing standardization over individual needs. The system was built to prepare students for an industrialized nation, but it has struggled to keep pace with the rapid technological, social, and economic changes of the 21st century (Schleicher, 2018).

Today, public education is at a critical juncture. Despite waves of reform and technological advancements, the delivery model remains stagnant. The subjects taught—reading, writing, and arithmetic—have barely evolved, even though the world students live in is drastically different (OECD, 2022). We continue to operate schools like the Flintstones in an era that demands the innovation of the Jetsons. The need for modernization is urgent, and the time for change is now. We all have a role to play in advocating for this change, and the urgency of this need should motivate us to act.

The fundamental question is this: Are we ready to leave behind the outdated public education model and create a future-ready system that prepares our children for the world ahead?

NOTES ON REFERENCES

This section is included in this manuscript to give readers a deeper understanding of the foundational research, historical perspectives, and contemporary insights that inform the book's narrative. Education is a dynamic field influenced by centuries of evolving philosophies, practices, and policies. The references selected for this work represent a carefully curated blend of seminal works, innovative techniques, and cutting-edge research from experts and institutions around the globe.

This section acknowledges the contributions of the authors, organizations, and studies cited and validates the book's arguments, offering readers a transparent view of the sources that shaped its ideas. Each reference is included for its unique contribution—whether as a historical cornerstone, an example of proven practices, or a vision for future educational innovations. By exploring the authors' qualifications, the organization's credibility, and the research's practical applications, readers can appreciate the rigor and thoughtfulness behind the proposals in this book.

This detailed exploration of references is an essential component of the manuscript, as it provides a roadmap for those who wish to delve deeper into the issues discussed. It also underscores the book's commitment to evidence-based recommendations, highlighting why these sources were integral to shaping a bold and transformative vision for the future of education.

References

1. **Barnett, W. S., et al. (2008). Educational Effects of the Tools of the Mind Curriculum:** This study is pivotal in understanding how structured, evidence-based early childhood curricula can

foster cognitive and social development. The randomized trial provides empirical backing for integrating tools and frameworks that enhance student self-regulation and readiness, which aligns with the book's emphasis on foundational skills in early education.

2. **Buck Institute for Education (2020). Project-Based Learning Handbook:** The Buck Institute's work on project-based learning (PBL) is a cornerstone for the book's advocacy for student-centered, inquiry-driven education. Their research demonstrates how PBL increases engagement and retention, supporting the argument for integrating real-world classroom problem-solving activities.

3. **Carnevale, A. P., et al. (2013). Recovery: Job Growth and Education Requirements Through 2020:** This report from Georgetown University underscores the evolving labor market demands, highlighting the critical need for education systems to align with workforce trends. It bolsters the book's call for career pathways and technical education to equip students with future-ready skills.

4. **Cubberley, E. P. (1920). The History of Education:** This historical perspective provides context for the book's critique of the industrial-era education model. Cubberley's exploration of the evolution of schooling underscores the need for radical modernization to meet current and future demands.

5. **Darling-Hammond, L., & Rothman, R. (2011). Teacher and Leader Effectiveness in High-Performing Education Systems:** This work emphasizes the importance of professional development and leadership in driving educational outcomes. It supports the book's argument for elevating teaching and leadership standards through the Master Teacher and Apprentice Model.

6. **Education Next (2018). Cronyism and Its Consequences in Public Education:** This article provides critical insights into governance issues, particularly the detrimental effects of cronyism on school leadership. It informs the book's discussion on the need for transparency and accountability in education systems.

7. **Epstein, J. L. (2018). School, Family, and Community Partnerships:** Epstein's framework for building meaningful collaborations between schools and families underpins the book's emphasis on parental engagement. It illustrates practical strategies for fostering partnerships that enhance student outcomes.

8. **Federal Ministry of Education and Research (2022).**

Germany's Dual Education System: This source highlights the success of Germany's dual education model, which combines academic learning with practical training. Its effectiveness in reducing youth unemployment aligns with the book's advocacy for integrated career pathways.

9. **Georgia Department of Education (2022). Move on When Ready Program:** Georgia's program offers a practical example of how flexible education pathways can prepare students for college and careers. It supports the book's call for similar initiatives to bridge gaps in readiness.

10. **Kuypers, L. (2011). The Zones of Regulation:** This curriculum is central to the book's focus on social-emotional learning. Kuypers' work offers a framework for teaching self-regulation and emotional control, which is essential for holistic student development.

11. **Mann, H. (1848). Annual Reports of the Secretary of the Board of Education of Massachusetts:** Horace Mann's foundational contributions to public education provide historical context for the book's critique of education systems' stagnation and call for visionary leadership.

12. **Mapp, K. L., & Kuttner, P. J. (2013). Partners in Education:** This dual capacity-building framework offers actionable strategies for engaging families as co-educators, supporting the book's argument for inclusive and collaborative educational practices.

13. **Means, B., & Murphy, R. (2014). The Effectiveness of Online and Blended Learning:** This meta-analysis validates the book's proposals for leveraging technology to enhance learning outcomes, demonstrating the efficacy of online and blended learning models.

14. **National PTA (2019). Family Engagement in Student Success:** This resource underscores the role of family involvement in driving student achievement, reinforcing the book's emphasis on creating meaningful opportunities for parental participation.

15. **Oakland Unified School District (2017). Restorative Justice in Oakland Schools:** Oakland's implementation of restorative justice practices provides evidence for alternative disciplinary approaches. The 60% reduction in suspensions cited in this study supports the book's advocacy for inclusive and supportive school cultures.

16. **OECD (2018). The Future of Education and Skills: Education 2030:** This report offers a forward-looking perspective on global

education trends, providing critical benchmarks and innovative strategies that inform the book's proposals for systemic reform.

17. **OECD (2022). Education at a Glance 2022**: This comprehensive set of indicators highlights disparities in education systems worldwide. Its data-driven insights support the book's calls for equity and innovation in education.

18. **RAND Corporation (2022). American Teacher Panel Survey Results:** This survey highlights the challenges faced by educators, particularly the prevalence of job-related stress. It underscores the need for systemic changes to support teacher well-being and efficacy.

19. **Sahlberg, P. (2015). Finnish Lessons 2.0:** Sahlberg's analysis of Finland's education system provides a blueprint for high-performing, equitable schools. It reinforces the book's call for reforms prioritizing teacher training and student autonomy.

20. **Schleicher, A. (2018). World Class: How to Build a 21st-Century School System:** Schleicher's insights into global education innovation provide a critical foundation for the book's arguments. His emphasis on adaptability and equity is echoed throughout the text.

21. **Swiss Federal Statistical Office (2022). Vocational Education and Training Statistics:** Switzerland's success in vocational education underscores the effectiveness of integrating academic and practical learning, a core theme of the book.

22. **Tennessee Department of Education (2022). Pathways to Prosperity Program:** Tennessee's program exemplifies how state-led initiatives can align education with workforce demands, supporting the book's vision for career-focused pathways.

23. **Wallace Foundation (2021). The Principal as Leader:** This research highlights the pivotal role of school leadership in shaping educational outcomes, providing empirical support for the book's emphasis on accountable and effective governance.

A diverse array of research and international examples supports this book's vision for transforming education. The sources cited provide both empirical evidence and insights into educational practices that have proven successful globally. Drawing from respected research bodies such as the OECD, the Buck Institute for Education, and the

RAND Corporation, these references underscore the book's advocacy for critical, data-backed educational reforms.

The sources are selected for their direct relevance to key concepts presented in each chapter, such as project-based learning, the Master Teacher model, and the integration of lifelong learning. Studies on educational systems in Finland, Germany, Singapore, and Switzerland illustrate how these nations have adopted adaptable, student-centered approaches to meet 21st-century demands, serving as benchmarks for reimagining U.S. education. These examples provide a solid foundation for the proposed innovations, demonstrating that transformative education models are feasible and successful.

By grounding each argument in well-established research, this book advocates change and ensures that each claim is rooted in a proven context, offering readers a compelling blueprint for the future of education.

CHAPTER 1
THE MORE THINGS CHANGE, THE MORE THEY STAY THE SAME

"TIMES CHANGE. WE NEED TO CHANGE AS WELL." ~ NELSON MANDELA

Picture that one-room schoolhouse in colonial America. A single teacher stands before a group of children of varying ages, guiding them through lessons. The objective was straightforward—to promote obedience and basic literacy. Fast-forward to today, and while the tools have evolved from slates to digital projectors, the essence of the classroom experience remains remarkably similar (Cubberley, 1920).

Students are grouped by age, seated in rows, and passively receiving information as a teacher leads instruction from the front of the room. Despite significant technological advancements and societal shifts, the core structure of education remains rooted in methods from centuries ago, a static system struggling to adapt to modern demands (OECD, 2022).

The One-Room Schoolhouse Legacy

While we like to believe that education has dramatically advanced since the days of the one-room schoolhouse, the reality is more complex. How we organize and deliver education today remains closely tied to those early, simplistic models. In many classrooms, students are grouped by age rather than abilities. This age-based grouping forces advanced learners to idle, often missing opportunities for deeper exploration of subjects, while struggling students are left behind, unable to keep pace. (Sahlberg, 2015).

Differentiated instruction is often proposed to address the varying student ability levels within a single classroom. Differentiated instruction is an educational framework that encourages teachers to tailor lessons to meet each student's learning needs, styles, and readiness levels. This approach aims to provide all students—advanced, average, and struggling—with meaningful, appropriately challenging learning experiences. However, despite its widespread mention in educational policy and rhetoric, genuine differentiation is challenging to implement effectively on a broad scale. It requires substantial training, resources, and support, which many educators lack due to time constraints, limited resources, and the demands of standardized testing. As a result, the promise of differentiated instruction often falls short, leaving many classrooms operating in ways that still resemble the uniform, one-size-fits-all approach of earlier times (Sahlberg, 2015; Tomlinson, 2001).

While technology has made significant inroads into the classroom, its potential to revolutionize learning has yet to be fully harnessed. Teachers often continue to lead from the front, delivering lessons in mass to students expected to absorb information unvaryingly without adapting the content to individual learning paces or styles. This approach overlooks the diverse needs of today's students, who require more interactive, personalized learning experiences to stay engaged and achieve more profound understanding. Such traditional methods reflect a lingering attachment to the priorities of a period far gone, which valued efficiency, standardization, and conformity over creativity and critical thinking. As a result, technology's role is often reduced to a supplementary tool rather than a transformative force, missing opportunities to create flexible, student-centered environments that cultivate the skills needed for success in today's complex world (Means & Murphy, 2014; Schleicher, 2018).

These factors underscore a persistent gap between modern education's goals and classroom realities. A fundamental shift is needed to bridge this divide—one that moves beyond traditional methods and embraces personalized, flexible learning environments. By fully integrating differentiated instruction and harnessing technology's potential, schools can more effectively address the diverse needs of all students, creating pathways for more meaningful engagement and enhanced learning outcomes.

Subjects Stuck in Time

Though nearly every sector has undergone significant transformations in the digital era, public school curricula remain stubbornly traditional. Foundational learning subjects still dominate the school day, much like the 19th century. New subjects—coding, digital literacy, and others—are introduced but often taught in isolation, disconnected from real-world applications and interdisciplinary problem-solving (OECD, 2022).

Take history, for example. In the 1800s, students memorized facts and dates, and many classrooms still follow this outdated model today. While more diverse perspectives have been incorporated, the focus remains on rote memorization, with little attention paid to fostering perilous thinking or connecting historical lessons to contemporary issues (Sahlberg, 2015). The introduction of technology in education has yet to shift this underlying approach significantly. Instead of simply listing dates and events, meaningful learning in history would invite students to engage with primary sources, participate in debates, and analyze historical events through various lenses, such as political, economic, and social contexts. Lessons could involve interactive timelines, digital simulations, or even role-playing scenarios to immerse students in the experiences of different historical periods. This active approach, supported by technology, would emphasize critical thinking, making historical events relevant to students' lives by connecting past lessons to current events and encouraging them to draw parallels, form opinions, and propose solutions to modern issues based on historical insights (Means & Murphy, 2014).

The Factory Model of Education: A Lasting Influence

The Industrial Revolution's factory education model has persisted mainly due to its foundational emphasis on standardized practices, which provided a practical, scalable approach to educating large groups. Initially, this model was designed to support the industrial workforce, emphasizing punctuality, routine, and uniformity to prepare students for structured, hierarchical work environments. The system's rigid structure—characterized by set schedules, age-based groupings, and uniform curricula—allowed for predictable, easily managed schooling that could be replicated across communities.

Its endurance in modern education reflects how deeply these practices are embedded within school infrastructure, where systems prioritize order, measurable outcomes, and streamlined processes. Such a model is convenient for administration and aligns with traditional student assessment and accountability methods. However, this emphasis on regularity does not align with today's educational goals, which require adaptable, diverse approaches to cultivate independent thinkers and lifelong learners rather than simply instilling skills for routine tasks.

The world has moved far beyond the industrial age, yet the education system still echoes these outdated priorities. School days remain rigidly structured, divided into periods marked by bells, much like factory shifts. Bureaucratic pressures and an entrenched reliance on standardized testing further inhibit innovation and creativity in both teaching and learning. This structure, focused on compliance and uniformity, constrains opportunities for students to engage in flexible, dynamic problem-solving—skills crucial for thriving in today's global, knowledge-based economy. Instead of fostering adaptability and independent thinking, the system often limits students to predictable routines, hindering their readiness for a world that values creativity and complex reasoning.

Stagnation Across Generations

Each generation of students has been shaped by distinct societal influences that impact their expectations, learning styles, and needs. However, education has remained rooted in its genesis, misaligned with the realities of today's world. Recognizing how each generation's unique context affects learning makes it clear that the current educational structures do not sufficiently prepare students for their rapidly evolving futures.

Traditionalists (born before 1945) grew up in an era of limited technological access, during which radio, print, and in-person interaction were primary modes of communication. Education for Traditionalists focused on memorization, obedience, and preparing students for industrial or clerical jobs, reflecting the societal priorities of their time. Our current educational delivery model fit this era by prioritizing discipline and order for jobs requiring consistent, mechanical tasks over innovation and adaptability.

Baby Boomers (1946-1964) experienced a period of post-war economic expansion, civil rights movements, and the beginnings of technological advancements. Although classrooms during this time remained teacher-centered, the curriculum began expanding to reflect social issues, especially in higher education. Baby Boomers were still subject to structured, hierarchical schooling, but the focus shifted to developing informed citizens as the U.S. economy moved towards white-collar jobs. While beneficial for this generation, the education system still emphasized conformity and discipline over creative thinking or digital literacy, skills that would later become crucial.

Generation X (1965-1980) grew up in an era of cultural shifts and early digital technology, such as personal computers and video games. Schools remained primarily traditional, with standardized testing becoming more prominent and tracking systems directing students into distinct academic or vocational paths. This generation saw the rise of dual-income families, making adaptability and self-reliance essential traits for these students. However, the educational system failed to capitalize on these emerging traits, focusing instead on rigid curricula and sorted learning, with little space for fostering self-directed exploration.

Millennials (1981-1996) came of age in a world where technology, especially the internet, was becoming central to everyday life. Millennials saw the rise of digital communication, social media, and a globalized economy that valued soft skills and interdisciplinary knowledge. Nevertheless, in schools, many were still educated in classrooms that did not fully integrate digital tools or encourage critical thinking skills to the extent their world demanded. Although some schools began using computers and introducing online resources, the underlying methods of instruction remained outdated. As a result, Millennials entered the workforce, often underprepared for the realities of a fast-paced, digital environment, needing to learn adaptability independently.

Generation Z (1997-2012) are true digital natives who grew up with the internet, smartphones, and social media as constants. They are accustomed to interactive, on-demand, and personalized experiences, yet many classrooms still employ lecture-based instruction, requiring passive listening and standardized testing. The gap between their daily digital interactions and their classroom experiences creates a disconnect, as Generation Z students are used to gathering information instantly and engaging in collaborative problem-solving online. The traditional, segmented approach of school subjects often feels arbitrary to a generation that sees interconnected, real-world issues play out on global platforms. Consequently, the rigid schooling structures often fail to engage them in the critical thinking and collaborative skills they innately use outside school.

Generation Alpha (2013-present) is growing in artificial intelligence, advanced automation, and immersive technology. These young learners will be expected to thrive in a job market with many roles that do not yet exist, requiring skills in creativity, flexibility, and critical analysis. They are becoming familiar with virtual assistants, augmented reality, and interactive learning apps from an early age, setting high expectations for interactive, tailored educational experiences. However, traditional classrooms are still based on static learning environments where subjects are isolated, assessment is standardized, and the curriculum is slow to adapt to technological advancements. For Generation Alpha, these structures may feel obsolete, as they are growing up with tools and platforms that make information retrieval and collaborative learning instantaneous and engaging.

Each generation has needed an education that resonates with its context, yet the current system, built on principles of homogeneousness and standardization, continues to limit the potential of today's learners. The system's inability to evolve with society's advancements hinders students' development of the essential skills needed in a world of rapid change, digital interconnectivity, and complex global challenges. Today's students require an educational approach that adapts as readily as the technology they use, fosters their natural curiosity, and prepares them for a future where they must innovate, collaborate, and think judgmentally.

Breaking Free: The Need for Change

The need to move beyond the Industrial-era education model has never been more urgent. As society evolves, so must our approach to preparing future generations. Incremental reforms—such as adding technology or shifting to more student-centered methods—have provided valuable insights but lack the transformative impact needed for today's world.

Education must prioritize skills that align with the demands of a modern workforce and society. We need a system that nurtures adaptability, creativity, and critical thinking—qualities that enable students to thrive in a complex, globalized environment. Schools must move from standardized instruction to dynamic, project-based learning where students actively solve real-world problems, collaborate with peers, and develop resilience.

This shift requires reimagining the curriculum, classroom structure, and teaching roles. Teachers should be empowered as facilitators and mentors, guiding students through exploration and encouraging intellectual curiosity. Assessment methods should evolve to measure growth in critical skills, focusing less on what to think and more on students' ability to apply their learning to novel challenges.

The opportunity for educational transformation is within reach. With a bold, forward-thinking vision, we can reshape public education to equip students for the future, fostering academic success and the skills essential for lifelong learning and global citizenship. The time to act is now, building a system that aligns with a new era's needs.

CHAPTER 2
Education at a Crossroads: The U.S. is Losing Ground

"There comes a time when you must choose between turning the page and closing the book." ~ Anonymous

The United States, once a beacon of educational excellence, now faces a daunting reality. We need to catch up. The cracks in our education system are widening, and the futures of millions of children are at risk. This educational decline has far-reaching consequences—not only affecting individual students' prospects but also threatening our nation's security and competitiveness on the global stage (Schleicher, 2018).

One clear example is cybersecurity. As cyber threats increase, we face a shortage of qualified professionals to protect critical infrastructure. According to recent reports, the United States has hundreds of thousands of unfilled cybersecurity positions due partly to a lack of rigorous STEM education in K-12 systems. This talent gap leaves our government, healthcare, and financial systems more vulnerable to international cyber-attacks, compromising national security.

Another example is in technology and innovation. Countries like China and India are making significant strides in artificial intelligence, biotechnology, and renewable energy—fields requiring a highly educated workforce with strong problem-solving skills and technical expertise. As the U.S. continues to lag in producing graduates proficient in these areas, we risk ceding leadership in critical technologies. Without a solid educational foundation, our ability to innovate and remain economically competitive weakens, ultimately affecting the nation's prosperity and geopolitical influence.

The choices we make now will determine whether we can reclaim our leadership in education or continue on a path that leaves our students unready for the challenges of tomorrow.

The Numbers Don't Lie: A Global Perspective

The most recent data from the Program for International Student Assessment (PISA) offers a sobering reminder of how far the U.S. has slipped in global rankings. In the 2022 results published by the Organization for Economic Co-Operation and Development (OECD), an intergovernmental organization with 38 member countries created to stimulate economic progress and world trade, the United States scored 465 in mathematics, below the global of 472. In contrast, countries like Japan and Singapore scored 527 and 564, respectively, highlighting a substantial gap in math proficiency. Estonia also outperformed the U.S. with a score of 523, reflecting the effectiveness of its educational reforms. While only 7% of U.S. students demonstrate advanced proficiency in math, over 30% of students in Singapore and nearly 20% in Japan achieved advanced levels (OECD, 2022). By comparison, more than a third of American students struggle with basic tasks like comparing distances or converting prices, indicating that the U.S. is falling significantly behind countries prioritizing critical thinking and applied math skills in their curricula.

These numbers are not just statistics—they underscore a significant and widening gap between U.S. students and their international peers and highlight the areas in which our current system is failing. For example, students in Singapore outscore Americans by over 100 points on the PISA scale, consistently demonstrating advanced skills in problem-solving and analytical reasoning (OECD, 2022). Japanese students, scoring roughly 60 points higher than their U.S. counterparts, are educated in systems that prioritize conceptual understanding and critical thinking, setting them up for success in fields demanding complex math and science skills (OECD, 2022; Sahlberg, 2015). Estonia, with scores around 58 points above the United States, has redesigned its education system to emphasize digital literacy and autonomous learning, preparing its students to excel academically, innovate, and adapt to the modern workforce (Schleicher, 2018). By contrast, American students are confined to a system that prioritizes compliance, memorization, and standardized testing, leaving them less equipped with the comprehension and problem-solving skills essential for success in today's economy (Darling-Hammond & Rothman, 2011). This divide reflects different academic achievements and a profound disparity in preparedness for future challenges.

A Broken System: How Our Children Are Suffering

The failures of the U.S. education system are particularly stark in low-income communities, where students face overwhelming barriers to success. Underfunded schools have more severe challenges: classrooms are overcrowded, teachers are overworked, and resources are scarce. The impact on Black, Hispanic, and low-income students is devastating. These children are left behind, and their opportunities are limited by systemic inequities that widen the achievement gap year after year (OECD, 2022). Rather than acting as the great equalizer, education in America perpetuates poverty cycles and reinforces socioeconomic divides, leaving many of these students to be relegated to the permanent underclass in one of the highest wage-earning nations in the world.

In affluent districts, students may have access to the latest technology, rigorous curricula, and a wealth of resources, yet they are often confined to rigid, test-driven learning models. Though privileged in comparison, these students do not realize their full potential due to an education system that values scores over understanding (Means & Murphy, 2014).

This is not just a question of academic achievement but a crisis of opportunity. When students from disadvantaged backgrounds fail to receive the education they deserve, their ability to break free from poverty diminishes, and their chances for upward mobility disappear. Instead of closing these gaps, the education system exacerbates them (Schleicher,

2018). Moreover, rigid education models stifle even privileged students, limiting their potential by emphasizing rote learning and standardized testing over creativity, inquiry, and independent thought. At the same time, those in elite schools may experience intense pressure to conform to narrow academic pathways, leaving little room for exploration in areas like the arts, entrepreneurship, or global citizenship.

The Global Race We Are Losing: Lessons from Abroad

Other nations are pulling ahead by embracing innovative approaches that align with the demands of the 21st century. Singapore, for instance, has transformed its education system into a global model by prioritizing teacher professional development and instilling problem-solving skills in students from an early age (Darling-Hammond & Rothman, 2011). Teachers undergo extensive training to adapt to evolving educational needs and are encouraged to foster active learning environments. Singapore's curriculum emphasizes collaborative projects, where students work in teams to solve real-world issues, and problem-based learning activities, which prompt students to explore solutions to complex questions relevant to their communities. Additionally, design thinking workshops and innovation labs allow students to develop creativity and critical thinking, encouraging them to experiment with ideas and work through challenges in collaborative settings (Means & Murphy, 2014). Through these methods, Singapore nurtures a generation of adaptable thinkers prepared for the dynamic demands of a global economy.

Another global leader in education, Japan, has embraced a culture of collective responsibility for student success. During the COVID-19 pandemic, Japan's educators went to extraordinary lengths to ensure no child was left behind, even going door-to-door to deliver educational materials and support (OECD, 2022). This dedication reflects a fundamental difference in how education is viewed—not just as a system but as a societal responsibility.

And despite its small size and limited resources, Estonia has built one of the best education systems in the world by focusing on digital literacy and student autonomy and reducing the emphasis on standardized testing (Schleicher, 2018). Estonia's approach is one of flexibility and innovation, which are sorely lacking in the U.S. education system. Their model offers a glimpse of what is possible when education adapts to meet the needs of a digital, interconnected world (OECD, 2022).

The U.S. at a Standstill: Stuck in the Past

The stark contrast between these international success stories and the U.S. education system raises a critical question: What happened to America's role as an educational leader? Our schools continue to operate on outdated models designed for a world that no longer exists.

Overwhelmed by bureaucratic demands and a fixation on standardized testing, administrators are too often prevented from rethinking education for the digital age (Means & Murphy, 2014). Instead of fostering innovation, they are bogged down by compliance and regulation. As a result, American students are left unprepared for future challenges while countries like Singapore, Japan, and Estonia continue to invest in and modernize their education systems (Darling-Hammond & Rothman, 2011).

The Real Cost of a Failing System

The consequences of maintaining a failing education system are profound. American students need to catch up in crucial subjects like math and science. As a result, the U.S. is producing an increasingly ill-equipped workforce to compete in a global economy (OECD, 2022). In fields like STEM, where innovation and technical skills are paramount, the U.S. struggles to keep pace with countries that have embraced forward-thinking educational reforms (Sahlberg, 2015).

The U.S. must now rely on talent from abroad to fill many of these critical roles, a trend that underscores the shortcomings of our education system (Schleicher, 2018). Countries like Singapore and Finland produce graduates with the skills needed to excel in STEM fields, while U.S. schools fail to prepare students for these high-demand careers (Darling-Hammond & Rothman, 2011). Many American students, lacking adequate STEM training, are funneled into less specialized roles in fields like retail, food service, or administrative support, where opportunities for career growth and economic stability are limited. According to the Georgetown Center on Education and the Workforce, a lack of STEM preparation often restricts students' access to higher-paying, skill-based careers, leading them into lower-wage positions that offer fewer pathways for advancement (Carnevale, Smith & Strohl, 2013). This trend impacts individual career trajectories and places the country at a disadvantage in fields that drive global competitiveness and economic growth.

Beyond the economic implications, the education system's failure to serve all students perpetuates deep-seated inequities. Poor students, particularly students of color, are being left behind, and their limited access to quality education is entrenching them in generational poverty. This is more than just an education crisis; it is a moral crisis that speaks to the heart of America's values of equality and opportunity (OECD, 2022).

The Crossroads: A Choice for the Future

The U.S. education system is at a critical juncture. We face a clear choice: continue down a path of mediocrity, where our students must fight to prepare for a globalized world, or take bold action to embrace innovation and collaboration. Singapore, Japan, and Estonia have shown us that education systems can be transformed by prioritizing flexibility, creativity, and student-centered learning.

The question is: Will we adapt to the future and reclaim our leadership in education, or will we remain stuck in the past, failing the very students who will shape the world of tomorrow?

CHAPTER 3
Breaking the Chains: The Challenges Holding Schools Back

"We must prepare students for their future, not our past." ~ Ian Jukes

Public education in the United States faces deep-rooted challenges that extend beyond simple policy fixes. These are not isolated issues but symptoms of a system designed for a bygone era, no longer equipped to meet the needs of today's rapidly changing world. Whether it is the shortage of qualified teachers, unsafe learning environments, weak leadership, or the growing disconnect between K-12 education and higher education, it is clear that incremental reforms will not suffice. A comprehensive overhaul is necessary to create an education system that prepares students for the future.

Teacher Scarcity and Respect: A Crisis in the Making

The shortage of qualified teachers in the U.S. has reached critical levels, with states like Arizona and Oklahoma struggling to fill thousands of teaching positions. In some cases, schools are left with no choice but to hire underqualified individuals. This teacher scarcity is not just about filling vacancies—it reflects a profession in crisis. Low pay, inadequate professional development, and increasing demands have made teaching less attractive, leading to high turnover and burnout. The RAND Corporation, an American nonprofit global policy think tank, conducted a 2022 survey revealing that 73% of teachers report frequent job-related stress, compared to 35% of other working adults.

This crisis highlights a deeper issue: the erosion of respect for the teaching profession. Teachers face stagnant wages that lag behind those of other professionals with similar levels of education, forcing many to work second jobs or leave the field entirely to make ends meet. According to a report from the Economic Policy Institute, teachers earn about 20% less than comparable professionals, a gap that has only widened in recent years. In addition to low pay, teachers often experience overwhelming workloads, exacerbated by larger class sizes and added responsibilities beyond instruction, such as administrative tasks and testing preparation. Professional autonomy has also eroded, with teachers frequently mandated to follow rigid curricula focused on standardized testing rather than creative, student-centered learning. Many educators feel they are seen as mere policy implementers rather than skilled professionals with valuable insights into their students' needs. To rebuild the education system, we must begin by restoring dignity and value to teaching through better compensation, continuous professional development, and greater professional autonomy. Teachers are at the heart of education reform, and addressing their needs is essential for any attempts at transformation to succeed.

School Culture and Safety: Learning in the Shadow of Fear

For many students, school is no longer the safe and supportive environment it once was. Incidents of violence, bullying, and mental health crises are on the rise, especially in schools within high-poverty areas, where resources are scarce and students often face compounding societal challenges. Factors such as inadequate funding, understaffing, and overworked faculty make it difficult for these schools to foster the positive cultures needed to counteract external pressures, leading to students feeling disconnected and unsupported.

The consequences are stark: students disengage from learning, academic performance suffers, and schools lose their ability to function as true centers of growth and safety (Schleicher, 2018). Without sufficient counseling services, extracurricular activities, or safe spaces within schools, students may turn to social media, peer groups, or even gang affiliations for the sense of belonging and support they lack in the classroom. Studies by the National Center for Education Statistics (NCES) report that bullying and violence are primary reasons for absenteeism and eventual dropout, as students increasingly perceive school as a hostile environment rather than a pathway to a brighter future.

Compounding these issues, students struggling with mental health challenges often find limited resources and support at school, as counselors are overwhelmed with caseloads far exceeding recommended limits. In many cases, this leads students to self-medicate or turn to risky behaviors as coping mechanisms, further pulling them away from education. To effectively support student well-being, schools must prioritize mental health services, foster inclusive communities, and address root causes like poverty and violence that impact school culture.

Addressing the challenges of today's students requires more than simply managing issues like bullying or absenteeism; it demands a more dedicated commitment to fostering a supportive, inclusive school culture. Schools prioritizing social-emotional learning (SEL)—a framework that teaches students to understand and manage their emotions, set positive goals, show empathy, and build healthy relationships—are making strides in behavior management and improving academic outcomes. Social-emotional learning helps students develop skills like empathy, resilience, and self-regulation, which are crucial for navigating conflicts, engaging positively with peers, and remaining invested in their education.

One practical approach gaining traction is restorative justice, a set of practices designed to help students take accountability for their actions while promoting healing within the school community. Instead of focusing solely on punishment, restorative justice encourages dialogue, understanding, and conflict resolution. For example, schools implementing restorative practices in Oakland saw remarkable success, including a 60% reduction in suspensions. These practices included student-led mediation sessions, peer accountability circles, and community service projects that encouraged students to make amends and understand the impact of their behavior (Oakland Unified School District, 2017). By prioritizing SEL and restorative justice, schools create a climate where students feel valued and safe, reducing the likelihood of disruptive behavior and fostering an environment conducive to academic success.

Research from the OECD (2022) further supports these findings, indicating that schools emphasizing student well-being and SEL report fewer behavioral issues and improved attendance and engagement. This holistic approach goes beyond merely managing surface-level challenges, helping to create a foundation of trust, respect, and mutual support essential for academic and personal growth.

Additionally, many schools have successfully implemented strategies to reinforce this positive shift. Schools prioritizing social-emotional learning and student well-being show measurable improvements in behavior and academic achievement, illustrating that prioritizing student well-being is not just a compassionate choice but essential for fostering academic success (OECD, 2022).

Leadership, Governance, and Cronyism: Barriers to Progress

Effective leadership is essential for fostering meaningful change in education. Yet, school and district leaders are too often more focused on managing public image, engaging in cronyism, and prioritizing optics over outcomes. Research consistently demonstrates that school leadership is second only to teaching in its impact on student learning, emphasizing the critical role of principals and district administrators in shaping academic success (Wallace Foundation, 2021). Despite this, many leaders prioritize appearance over genuine improvement, leading to superficial reforms that look promising on paper but yield little measurable impact on student achievement.

Adding to the problem is the issue of cronyism within school leadership, where individuals are appointed to positions based on personal connections rather than qualifications or demonstrated expertise. Cronyism reduces accountability, as leaders often surround themselves with allies who may prioritize loyalty over educational effectiveness. A study by Educational Leadership found that districts impacted by cronyism experienced significantly lower staff morale and higher turnover, directly hindering school stability and educational outcomes (Sahlberg, 2015). Staff members often recognize cronyism through repeated hiring or promotion patterns favoring insiders over qualified external candidates. This culture of favoritism perpetuates ineffective leadership practices and diminishes the school's capacity to adapt to necessary reforms (Education Next, 2018).

This lack of accountability and expertise often leads to misguided priorities. For instance, some leaders focus on high-visibility projects, such as technology upgrades or facility renovations, designed to enhance public perception rather than address core educational needs. According to the OECD, such initiatives may create temporary favorable impressions but have limited impact on student outcomes if not integrated into a broader improvement strategy that includes meaningful support for instruction and curriculum. These projects are frequently implemented without a holistic plan, diverting resources from essential areas like reducing class sizes, increasing teacher support, or improving curriculum quality.

Moreover, the Wallace Foundation found that many school leaders launch "student-centered" programs to appeal to stakeholders. However, without adequate planning, resources, or teacher training, these programs often lack the infrastructure necessary to succeed. This optics-focused approach leaves teachers underprepared to implement these initiatives, ultimately failing to enhance student learning.

The emphasis on appearances, cronyism, and ineffective resource allocation reflects a troubling disconnect between educational leadership and the genuine needs of students and teachers. To create meaningful, lasting change, educational leaders must move beyond superficial improvements and instead implement transparent hiring practices, prioritize accountability, and commit to evidence-based strategies that support practical educational goals. Ensuring leadership is driven by qualified, outcome-oriented professionals—rather than political allies—will help align school priorities with the long-term interests of students and communities.

Partnerships and Alignment with Higher Education: Closing the Gap

The gap between K-12 education and higher education requirements or technical careers is a significant challenge in the current education system. Many high school graduates lack critical thinking, problem-solving, and advanced literacy and numeracy skills, leaving them underprepared for the rigor of college coursework. This lack of preparedness often results in high rates of remedial classes and college dropouts. Programs like Georgia's "Move on When Ready" and Tennessee's "Pathways to Prosperity" aim to bridge this gap by offering students the chance to earn college credits and acquire technical skills while still in high school, fostering academic and career readiness. These initiatives help students build competencies essential for success in both college and the workforce, such as hands-on experience, project-based learning, and exposure to industry practices (Georgia Department of Education, 2022; Tennessee Department of Education, 2022). However, such forward-thinking programs are still exceptions rather than the norm, leaving many students without a clear path to post-secondary success (Sahlberg, 2015).

To address these gaps on a larger scale, establishing more robust partnerships between K-12 education, higher education, and industry is essential for equipping students with the skills needed after high school. Germany's dual education system, which blends classroom learning with practical trade training, provides a model that could significantly enhance U.S. education. Developing clearer pathways from high school to college or the workforce can prepare students more effectively for the modern economy's demands and complexities (Schleicher, 2018).

Conclusion: The System is Broken—It is Time to Replace It

Public education's challenges are not isolated problems but symptoms of a fundamentally flawed system. Teacher shortages, unsafe school environments, weak leadership, cronyism, and a lack of alignment with higher education all point to one conclusion: the current system is broken beyond repair. Incremental reforms will not suffice.

It is time to replace this outdated, industrial-era model with one that values efficient leadership, transparent governance, well-trained teachers, and real-world readiness. By embracing innovation, accountability, and transparency, we can build an education system that is fit for the 21st century and capable of allowing every student to succeed.

CHAPTER 4
Glimpse Into the Future: The School of Tomorrow

"The future belongs to those who believe in the beauty of their dreams." ~ Eleanor Roosevelt

In the past, our schools were built to conform to rigid, hierarchical systems designed to produce compliant workers for factories, but today's world demands something far more dynamic. As technology advances, economies globalize, and the challenges of the 21st century unfold before us, our schools must transform in ways that reflect these realities. This chapter presents a vision of what that future could look like: a school system built on the principles of innovation, collaboration, and equity, where the focus is not on compliance but on helping every student realize their full potential (Schleicher, 2018).

Governance for Change: Boards as Ambassadors, Not Politicians

The future of school governance begins with a profound shift in the role of Boards of Education. In this new model, school boards function not as political battlegrounds or enforcers of old traditions, but as ambassadors for innovation. They work through the district superintendent to ensure resources are allocated efficiently, relying on professional expertise rather than personal agendas. No longer swayed by dissatisfied voices intent on preserving the status quo, boards are driven by strategic planning and a shared commitment to helping students thrive in an interconnected, rapidly evolving world. Their primary goal is to support the new educational vision, ensuring the system adapts to future demands (Sahlberg, 2015).

Through their work with district leadership, school boards help shape a new kind of school system that is dynamic, inclusive, and driven by evidence-based practices. They advocate for schools that foster creativity, innovation, and personalized learning. Their role is not to micromanage or interfere with professional educational decisions, but to champion the mission of the future school, ensuring it aligns with the needs of the community and the students it serves (Schleicher, 2018)

The Master Teacher and Apprentice Model: A New Framework for Educators

The Master Teacher and Apprentice Model is at the core of this transformed educational structure, drawing on the concept of apprenticeships but modernized to meet today's needs. In this model, Master Teachers are highly trained, skilled professionals who serve not only as instructors but also as mentors, curriculum designers, and leaders across multiple schools, helping shape the educational experience at a systemic level (OECD, 2022). These educators are valued for their expertise and compensated accordingly, and they are recognized as the architects of quality instruction. Their impact is extended through virtual platforms, which allow them to connect with students in under-resourced or geographically isolated areas, ensuring consistent, top-tier education across various sites.

In this collaborative approach, the Master Teacher leads lessons virtually on a standardized schedule across multiple classrooms. This structure enables them to deliver uniform, rigorous instruction to all students while maintaining a consistent level of educational quality. Onsite, Apprentice Teachers support this model by providing hands-on student assistance, managing classroom dynamics, upholding behavior standards, and maintaining academic integrity. Acting as on-the-ground guides, Apprentice Teachers gain critical experience in classroom management and instructional techniques while gradually developing their skills under the direct mentorship of Master Teachers. This partnership is designed to create a pipeline of future educators, nurturing aspiring teachers into the Master Teacher role and ensuring a continuous flow of highly qualified professionals.

International models have demonstrated the efficacy of such a system. For example, Finland and the Netherlands have effectively used team-based instruction, combining virtual expert teaching with onsite support to optimize student engagement and learning outcomes (OECD, 2022). These systems ensure that students receive not only high-quality instruction but also local support tailored to their needs, creating a well-rounded learning environment. Similarly, Germany's dual education system provides a structured pathway for apprentices to advance, blending real-world classroom experience with formal training (Sahlberg, 2015). This dual focus on practical and academic growth equips Apprentice Teachers with the competencies they need to lead classrooms independently.

The Master Teacher and Apprentice Model also addresses the challenges of teacher shortages by maximizing the expertise of experienced educators while providing a structured pathway for apprentices to grow. Schools can utilize available staff effectively, even those still working toward full certification, by placing them in supportive roles that allow them to contribute meaningfully to student learning while gaining essential skills. This approach is particularly valuable in under-resourced areas, where having access to a Master Teacher's expertise—supplemented by the presence of an Apprentice—creates a balanced, supportive learning environment that might otherwise be out of reach.

Ultimately, the Master Teacher and Apprentice Model elevates the teaching profession, restoring dignity and purpose to the role of educators by treating them as essential, highly skilled professionals. Master Teachers become exemplars of the teaching craft, and Apprentice Teachers have visible, respected models of excellence to aspire toward. This structure not only supports the immediate needs of students and schools but also ensures a steady, sustainable pipeline of future Master Teachers ready to lead the next generation. By fostering professional growth, elevating instructional quality, and creating sustainable pathways to teaching, this model redefines the role of educators and strengthens the foundation of education itself.

Early Mastery and Modular Learning for Elementary Students

One of the most transformative aspects of the future school model lies in how we approach the education of elementary-aged children, particularly in grades Pre-K through 2nd grade. This stage of schooling becomes a critical foundation where students are no longer grouped by age but by ability and mastery. The goal is to ensure that every child leaves this phase with solid literacy and numeracy skills, fully prepared to excel in more complex disciplines in the later grades.

In this new model, students in grades Pre-K through second progress through learning modules primarily focusing on reading and math. These modules are designed to break down content into manageable chunks, allowing students to progress at their own pace based on their mastery of each skill. For instance, in reading, children begin with basic literacy skills such as alphabet recognition and phonemic awareness, gradually advancing toward more complex tasks like reading comprehension and fluency. In math, students start with basic computation and problem-solving, building toward more complicated concepts like patterns, spatial awareness, and early arithmetic.

Science and Social Studies are integrated into reading and math modules, allowing students to engage with these subjects in contextually relevant ways. For example, reading comprehension tasks might involve passages about environmental science or history, while math exercises might include measuring objects in nature or exploring geography through map-based problems. This interdisciplinary approach ensures that students begin thinking critically across various subject areas, even at an early age.

Utilizing virtual Master Teachers at the elementary level provides a practical, high-quality alternative when schools cannot staff qualified educators onsite. In cases where virtual instruction is preferable to assigning nonqualified teachers, a virtual Master Teacher can lead engaging, interactive lessons, ensuring that students receive foundational guidance aligned with best teaching practices. Technology enables these virtual Master Teachers to connect with young learners through live video, interactive platforms, and digital tools, bringing structured, high-quality instruction to otherwise lacking classrooms.

In this model, children progress through the Pre-K through second learning modules based on their ability level, not age. This allows advanced learners to move forward without being held back by age-based grade structures, giving struggling students the time and support they need to succeed. By 3rd grade, all students are expected to have mastered the fundamentals of reading and math. At this point, they begin matriculating into more complex disciplines like science, social studies, and the arts, which are taught using the same project-based, hands-on structure as the upper grades.

International Context for Modular Learning

In this model, each elementary student's day is designed to foster self-directed learning, blending structured activities with independent modules that students complete at their own pace. Each day might begin with a session led by the Master Teacher, where students set personalized learning goals and review their progress. The classroom is divided into learning stations dedicated to core subjects like literacy, numeracy, and critical thinking, with each station offering modules and materials tailored to different levels of mastery. Students rotate through these stations, working on individualized tasks or small group activities with the Apprentice Teacher or teacher aide, who provides guidance and support as needed (Sahlberg, 2015; New et al. of Education, 2022).

For example, early readers might work on phonics with manipulatives or digital reading games in a literacy module, while advanced readers focus on comprehension exercises with more complex texts. In numeracy modules, younger students engage in counting and basic arithmetic, while those further along tackle problem-solving with real-world applications. Teachers and aides monitor progress, providing direct instruction when students struggle or encouraging peer collaboration for shared learning. The day concludes with a reflection period, where students discuss their accomplishments and set goals for the next day, reinforcing ownership and accountability in their learning (Darling-Hammond, 2020; OECD, 2018).

This approach, inspired by the educational models of Finland and New Zealand, promotes a learning environment that balances guidance with independence, enabling each student to develop at their own pace while building a solid academic foundation (OECD, 2022; Sahlberg, 2015).

Executive Functioning and Critical Thinking: Laying the Foundation for Future Success

In addition to the academic modules, executive functioning skills are embedded into the daily routines of Pre-K through second-grade students, supporting essential organizational skills, time management, and self-regulation needed for later academic success. For example, in the United States, many schools introduce "morning check-ins," where students plan their day, set small goals, and review what they need to accomplish. Programs such as Tools of the Mind, used nationally, include activities that prompt young students to think ahead, monitor their progress, and reflect on their behavior. This model encourages children to create "play plans" during structured playtime, which outline their activities, fostering an early sense of goal-setting and self-regulation (Barnett et al., 2008).

Internationally, Finland's educational system incorporates executive functioning by emphasizing student-led routines that build these skills naturally. Finnish students, from a young age, are involved in organizing their learning environments, choosing tasks within structured frameworks, and transitioning independently between activities. This self-directed approach nurtures independence and time management, aligning with Finland's educational philosophy of fostering responsibility and self-control early in schooling (Sahlberg, 2015).

For students with intellectual disabilities, executive functioning is taught through more structured, incremental steps. For example, teachers use visual schedules and task lists to break assignments into manageable parts, ensuring students understand each step before moving on. In Canada, the Zones of Regulation program helps students with disabilities recognize and manage emotions, a key component of executive functioning that impacts self-control and decision-making. Through color-coded zones, students learn to identify their emotions and use coping strategies to stay on task, a practical approach in many inclusive classrooms (Kuypers, 2011).

These executive functioning skills are essential for all students, providing a foundation for academic achievement and personal growth, especially as tasks become more complex and independent in higher grades.

Daily critical thinking exercises are a core component of this model, designed to teach students from a young age how to analyze, apply, and synthesize information rather than rely solely on memorization. In the United States, programs like Project-Based Learning (PBL) engage students in real-world problem-solving tasks that require them to connect academic concepts to everyday scenarios. For instance, elementary students might explore environmental science by studying a local habitat, then brainstorm and implement ways to protect it, encouraging them to ask questions, assess options, and make evidence-based decisions. This hands-on, inquiry-driven approach nurtures critical thinking by engaging students directly with the material to foster curiosity and problem-solving skills (Buck Institute for Education, 2020).

Internationally, critical thinking is a significant focus in countries like

Singapore, where the education system emphasizes "thinking schools, learning nation" as a national vision. Singaporean students regularly participate in activities requiring them to use critical thinking skills, such as debate and group discussions, encouraging them to evaluate different perspectives and apply their knowledge practically. In Finland, students engage in collaborative tasks that require them to work as a team to solve real-world problems, such as designing sustainable community projects. Finnish educators often emphasize questions over answers, encouraging students to think deeply about "why" and "how" things work, thereby building cognitive flexibility and critical reasoning from an early age (Sahlberg, 2015).

For students with special educational needs, adapted critical thinking exercises are integrated through structured yet open-ended tasks that encourage exploration and reasoning. In Australia, for example, inclusive classrooms use programs like "STEAM Ahead", where students with intellectual disabilities are introduced to simple engineering challenges that promote reasoning and planning, helping them to build foundational critical thinking skills within their capabilities.

Through these exercises, students not only master academic subjects but also develop the mental agility and confidence to approach complex issues thoughtfully, equipping them with skills crucial for both higher education and real-world problem-solving.

Learning by Doing: A Curriculum Drenched in Experience

The curriculum of the future school is no longer confined to textbooks or static content delivery. Instead, it is work-based and experience-laden, emphasizing real-world learning through project-based tasks and hands-on activities. Lessons are designed to engage students in critical thinking, synthesis, analysis, and application of knowledge. Instead of teaching students what to think, the focus is on teaching them how to think—how to apply what they learn to solve real-world problems (OECD, 2022).

Students regularly participate in field trips, immersive experiences, and community projects that provide context to their learning. These experiences are not afterthoughts but integral parts of the curriculum. For example, students studying environmental science might spend a week working with local conservation groups, applying their classroom knowledge to protect ecosystems in their community. Technology plays a crucial role in facilitating these experiences, with virtual reality simulations, interactive labs, and global collaborations allowing students to explore new concepts and deepen their understanding (Schleicher, 2018).

International research strongly supports integrating project-based learning (PBL), with Finland leading the way in creative and collaborative educational practices. Finnish schools prioritize critical thinking and hands-on problem-solving over standardized testing, fostering an environment where students engage deeply with content. For example, a prominent study by Sahlberg (2015) highlights Finland's use of multidisciplinary projects known as "phenomenon-based learning," where students explore real-world themes—such as climate change or urban development—by integrating science, geography, history, and language studies. This approach promotes creativity and collaboration, encouraging students to research, discuss, and present solutions to complex issues, thereby developing their analytical and teamwork skills.

Research from the OECD (Schleicher, 2018) indicates that Finland's PBL approach significantly enhances student engagement and long-term knowledge retention. Finnish students are often tasked with projects like planning a sustainable community garden, which includes elements of math (budgeting and measurements), biology (plant selection and soil health), and social studies (community impact). Through such projects, students gain practical knowledge while building critical skills, equipping them to address future societal challenges effectively. This PBL model aligns with findings in international education research, showing that hands-on, collaborative learning experiences cultivate skills that standardized testing fails to measure, such as problem-solving, adaptability, and critical thinking.

Leadership Redefined: Coaching, Not Compliance

In this futuristic school model, leadership roles are no longer driven by compliance with state and federal mandates. Instead, leaders focus on creating equitable, efficient learning environments that meet the needs of all students. School leaders split their time between office days and coaching days, working closely with other site administrators, Master Teachers, and instructional support staff to continuously improve teaching practices and student outcomes (OECD, 2022).

The role of school principals and administrators shifts from being primarily managerial to becoming Instructional Coaches who support teachers in their professional growth. They guide Apprentice Teachers through their development, ensuring they have the tools and knowledge to become future Master Teachers. Leaders foster a culture of collaboration, where educators work together to solve challenges and innovate new teaching methods (Sahlberg, 2015).

By prioritizing equity and excellence, school leaders help create a system where every student, regardless of background or ability, can succeed. The focus is on providing high-quality education to all students, not just meeting compliance standards (Schleicher, 2018).

Coaching Days: From Spectators to Architects of Learning

As school leadership transforms from traditional management to active engagement in the classroom, Coaching Days emerge as a central element of this new vision. On Coaching Days, school leaders—principals, assistant principals, and instructional support staff—dedicate their time to learning walkthroughs and teacher development, focusing on continuous improvement in teaching practices and student outcomes.

These days, leaders are not behind desks or engaged in administrative tasks; instead, they are immersed in the instructional process, observing, coaching, and collaborating with teachers to refine instruction and foster student success.

Continuous Learning Walkthroughs: Leadership in Action

During Coaching Days, school leaders conduct learning walkthroughs, which involve visiting classrooms to gather evidence on teaching and learning. These walkthroughs are structured but flexible, focusing on key instructional priorities such as student engagement, critical thinking, and collaborative learning. The purpose of these walkthroughs is to provide formative feedback rather than evaluative judgments, offering teachers actionable insights on their practices.

Leaders observe classrooms, noting how lessons are delivered, how students interact with content, and how teaching strategies align with the school's improvement goals. This process includes gathering non-evaluative evidence, such as observing student tasks, teacher-student interactions, and the overall instruction flow. The goal is to identify areas of strength and opportunities for growth, creating a data-informed foundation for future coaching and professional development.

After the learning walkthroughs, leaders engage teachers in collaborative discussions. During these discussions, teachers reflect on what was observed, celebrate successes, and identify areas for improvement. These discussions are opportunities for shared learning and professional growth, fostering a culture of continuous improvement.

Triangulating Findings and Supporting Teachers

Following Coaching Days, leaders and instructional support staff collaborate to triangulate their findings from classroom observations. They analyze classroom patterns to identify trends, gaps, and areas where teachers need additional support. These collaborative sessions allow leaders to develop a unified approach to instructional improvement, ensuring that professional development is targeted and responsive to the needs of both teachers and students.

Based on these findings, leaders design professional development sessions that address specific challenges observed during walkthroughs. For example, suppose walkthrough data reveals students struggle with higher-order thinking tasks. In that case, the leadership team may organize workshops on strategies to promote critical thinking and problem-solving in the classroom. This approach ensures that professional learning aligns with real-time classroom needs, driving teacher and student growth.

The Role of Coaching in Teacher Development

Coaching Days extend beyond walkthroughs to include in-depth coaching sessions with teachers. These sessions focus on personalized support, where leaders work with teachers to fine-tune instructional practices, develop new strategies, and set goals for improvement. By fostering a supportive, growth-oriented environment, school leaders help teachers feel empowered to take risks, innovate, and continuously refine their craft.

Coaching also creates a space for peer learning, where teachers can observe each other's classrooms and engage in collaborative reflection. This peer observation model not only strengthens the instructional community within the school but also encourages teachers to share best practices and learn from one another.

External Partnerships and Pathways to Success

Another critical component of the new educational structure is the development of external partnerships offering state-approved student pathways. These partnerships create pipelines for students not interested in pursuing a traditional college education, guiding them toward livable-wage jobs with growth opportunities. These pathways, created in collaboration with industries and local businesses, allow students to gain technical skills and work experience while still in school (Sahlberg, 2015).

For example, a partnership with a local healthcare provider might offer students hands-on nursing or medical technology training, providing them a direct route to a well-paying job upon graduation. Similar programs could be developed with industries such as technology, engineering, or skilled trades, ensuring that students leave school with the skills and certifications needed to succeed in the workforce (Schleicher, 2018).

This approach has inspired models in countries such as Switzerland and Germany, where dual-education systems combine academic learning with apprenticeships, giving students a clear path from education to employment (Sahlberg, 2015).

Pathways to Every Field of Human Endeavor: The "Chance and Choice" Program

In this visionary educational model, pathways to every field of human endeavor become central to the curriculum and experience. This approach goes beyond simply preparing students academically—it gives them real, tangible opportunities to acquire certifications, gain work experience, and transition seamlessly into the workforce. These pathways are developed through partnerships with local businesses, industries, and school departments, providing students with multiple options based on their interests and passions.

The "Chance and Choice Program" is designed to offer students practical career opportunities starting at an early age. School departments such as Human Resources, Business and Finance, Technology, and Facility Maintenance are transformed into learning laboratories where students gain hands-on experience in real-world tasks. Under the guidance of Master Teachers and qualified professionals, students engage in meaningful work that teaches them the skills necessary for their chosen field and connects them directly to future employment opportunities within the school district or beyond.

Schools establish memorandums of understanding to formalize collaborations with local businesses ranging from small enterprises to Fortune 500 companies. These partnerships create state-approved pathways—coursework and training programs that align with industry standards—ensuring students graduate with the skills and credentials they need to succeed. Students can pursue certifications in areas such as technology, business management, facility operations, or any other trades, gaining academic credit and work experience that can lead to immediate employment.

Graduates of these programs would have the opportunity to work within the same school district that educated them, using their newly acquired skills to give back to their community while building their careers. For example, a student who completes a pathway in technology might return to the district as an IT specialist. At the same time, another who excels in business management could join the district's finance department.

This approach introduces trades and career options as early as elementary school, allowing children to explore various fields and identify their passions. By the time they reach high school, students can attend schools based on their interests, choose programs that align with their ambitions, and receive specialized instruction in those areas. These schools are not simply educational institutions but incubators for success, fostering the skills and experience necessary for students to thrive in their chosen fields.

The "Chance and Choice Program" recognizes that not all students will pursue traditional college pathways. For many, the opportunity to enter the workforce directly after high school—armed with certifications, experience, and connections to local industries—offers a viable and fulfilling option. This model empowers students to make informed choices about their futures, whether enrolling in college, starting a business, enlisting in the military, or stepping directly into the workforce.

International Context and Research

Germany's dual education system and Switzerland's Vocational Education and Training (VET) programs offer compelling examples of how blending classroom learning with hands-on work can lead to significant career success and economic mobility. In Germany, over 50% of young people participate in the dual system, combining classroom instruction with apprenticeships in engineering, manufacturing, and IT. Approximately 70% of graduates from this program secure employment in their chosen fields directly after training, creating a strong link between education and career success (Federal Ministry of Education and Research, 2022).

Similarly, Switzerland's VET system, which engages about two-thirds of Swiss students, provides a clear pathway to skilled employment. Swiss students can pursue apprenticeships in healthcare, finance, and information technology while earning a stipend, which helps offset education costs and reduces student debt. The VET system reports that over 90% of participants find employment within six months of completing their training, with many advancing into roles that offer high wages and career growth (Swiss Federal Statistical Office, 2022). These programs illustrate the potential of a well-structured, career-focused education system to support high employment rates, economic mobility, and skilled workforce development by integrating education directly with career opportunities.

Reimagining Testing and Student Assessment

In the future school, testing is no longer about picking winners and losers. Instead, it is a diagnostic tool to gauge students' thinking processes, helping teachers identify areas where students need support or acceleration. Tests assess higher-order thinking skills, such as analyzing, synthesizing, and applying knowledge in new situations (Schleicher, 2018).

Though intuitively understood as a tool for growth, testing is still not implemented this way in many schools despite overwhelming research supporting its potential. In an ideal system, testing is not punitive but formative, providing insights to guide teachers and students. When the majority of students struggle with a concept, it should be a signal for additional teacher support, professional development, and instructional adjustments. Conversely, when most students grasp the material, testing results should prompt opportunities for student remediation and immediate advancement, ensuring that no one is held back unnecessarily. This approach is supported by extensive brain science and child psychology research, highlighting that assessments should serve as pathways for improvement rather than barriers, fostering a learning environment where every student can thrive (OECD, 2022).

A New Role for Parents

In this new model, parents are active, essential partners in their children's educational journey, engaging in meaningful and manageable ways. Rather than relying on outdated expectations like attending every school event, schools now offer various flexible, impactful opportunities for parental involvement that accommodate busy schedules and diverse family backgrounds. Parents are invited to participate in digital platforms to monitor their child's progress in real-time, access resources for supporting learning at home, and communicate easily with teachers to stay informed on academic and behavioral milestones (Epstein, 2018).

For example, some schools have implemented "learning at home" initiatives, where parents are guided on reinforcing skills through everyday activities, like measuring ingredients for a recipe to strengthen math skills or discussing current events to encourage critical thinking. Schools might also facilitate parent-led workshops or online forums where parents can share insights and strategies, building a supportive community that benefits students and families. According to research by the National PTA (2019), these parent-led forums and workshops improve academic outcomes by promoting shared accountability and collaborative problem-solving.

Another effective strategy is parent-teacher-student conferences that go beyond traditional report card reviews. In this setting, parents collaborate with teachers and their children to set realistic goals and identify strengths and areas needing support. Schools that have adopted this model report greater parental satisfaction and engagement and improved student performance and motivation, as the conference format fosters a team-oriented approach to learning (Mapp & Kuttner, 2013).

Additionally, community involvement days allow parents to engage directly in their child's learning environment, such as career days, project exhibitions, or volunteer tutoring sessions. These interactions allow parents to contribute in ways that directly impact the learning process and give them insights into the curriculum and school culture. This shift from passive observation to active participation empowers parents and strengthens the school-family bond, which has been shown to boost student success significantly (Schleicher, 2018).

Conclusion: A Vision for the Future

This new school model offers a vision of what education could be: dynamic, inclusive, and forward-thinking. Highly skilled Master Teachers lead from the front, supported by Apprentice Teachers and instructional leaders, and students are given the tools they need to succeed in a rapidly changing world. External partnerships create clear pathways to employment while testing and assessment are used as tools for growth, not punishment (Schleicher, 2018).

This model is not just about innovation for its own sake—it is about creating an education system that prepares every student for success, whether enrolling in college, enlisting in the military, starting their own business, or entering the workforce. It recognizes the potential in every child and is committed to helping them achieve their dreams. By embracing these bold changes, we can build schools that reflect the needs of the 21st century and beyond, offering hope and opportunity to future generations.

CHAPTER 5
REIMAGINING THE FUTURE OF EDUCATION – INTEGRATION AND EVOLUTION

"THE ILLITERATE OF THE 21ST CENTURY WILL NOT BE THOSE WHO CANNOT READ AND WRITE, BUT THOSE WHO CANNOT LEARN, UNLEARN, AND RELEARN."
~ ALVIN TOFFLER

As the landscape of education evolves, it is essential to move beyond piecemeal reforms and embrace a cohesive, transformative model that addresses the multifaceted needs of students, teachers, and communities. This chapter synthesizes the pillars of innovation, collaboration, and adaptability, illustrating how each aspect of the educational ecosystem must work together to build a future-ready school system. Drawing from global examples, evidence-based practices, and cutting-edge pedagogical strategies, we explore the foundation for a school structure that prepares students to thrive in an interconnected, rapidly changing world.

Master and Apprentice Model: A Team-Based Approach to Teaching Excellence

At the core of this new structure is the Master and Apprentice Model, inspired by traditional apprenticeships but redesigned to meet the complexities of modern education. In this model, Master Teachers are highly trained educators equipped with specialized certifications and extensive experience, tasked with delivering high-quality instruction and mentoring Apprentice Teachers. This team-based model allows for a balance of virtual and onsite instruction, ensuring consistent quality across schools, especially in under-resourced areas (OECD, 2022).

Master Teachers connect with multiple classrooms via virtual platforms, allowing students across the district to benefit from their expertise. These teachers work closely with Apprentice Teachers onsite, who are working toward certification and developing classroom management and instructional skills. Drawing from Finland's team-teaching model, which emphasizes collaboration and peer mentorship, this structure enables teachers to focus on what they do best: teaching and mentoring (Sahlberg, 2015). The model builds a sustainable pipeline of highly skilled educators ready to meet the evolving demands of today's classrooms, fostering continuity in instructional quality and teacher development.

Assessment for Growth: Portfolios and Competency-Based Progression

Traditional grading systems often fail to capture the full scope of student learning, limiting the ability to assess deeper competencies such as critical thinking and creativity. In the School of Tomorrow, portfolios will replace traditional grading as a primary assessment tool. These portfolios include a diverse array of work products, from essays and presentations to real-world projects, showcasing students' abilities to synthesize information and apply knowledge in meaningful ways.

Master Teachers will evaluate these portfolios, assessing student progress based on competencies rather than rigid numerical grades. According to the Buck Institute for Education, project-based assessments, which allow students to demonstrate understanding through application, foster higher levels of engagement and retention (Buck Institute for Education, 2020). This system supports a personalized approach, encouraging students to take ownership of their learning while providing detailed feedback to guide their development. In Finland, similar models have shown significant improvements in student motivation and comprehension by prioritizing mastery over memorization (Schleicher, 2018).

Flexible, Student-Centered Learning Environments

To foster self-directed learning and support a range of activities, classrooms in the School of Tomorrow will incorporate flexible, modular spaces designed to support various learning styles and tasks. Drawing inspiration from biophilic design principles, classrooms will integrate natural elements such as plants, natural lighting, and outdoor learning areas, creating an environment that promotes well-being and cognitive engagement. Biophilic design, widely used in countries like Denmark and Japan, has been shown to reduce stress, improve focus, and enhance creativity, supporting both academic achievement and emotional well-being (Schleicher, 2018).

Classrooms will feature distinct activity zones tailored to specific tasks. For example, in New Zealand, classrooms often include zones for quiet study, collaboration, and hands-on activities. Students may move to a "research station" for independent work or a "collaboration corner" to discuss project ideas with peers, fostering autonomy and choice in their learning journey (Sahlberg, 2015). This flexible design ensures that students can engage in various learning experiences that meet their individual needs while maintaining a structured framework.

Real-World Learning: The Role of Community Partnerships

A key component of this evolved educational model is integrating real-world experiences into the curriculum through partnerships with local industries, businesses, and organizations. Inspired by Germany's dual-education system, students in the School of Tomorrow will have opportunities to gain hands-on experience in various fields. Partnerships with local companies, government agencies, and nonprofits will allow students to split their time between school and real-world environments, applying what they learn in the classroom to real-world scenarios.

This approach extends beyond traditional vocational paths, offering students experience in areas like environmental science, technology, healthcare, and digital arts. In Switzerland, nearly 70% of students participate in vocational education programs, leading to some of the highest youth employment rates in Europe (OECD, 2022). By creating clear pathways from education to career, the School of Tomorrow ensures that every student graduates with practical skills, real-world experience, and a clear vision for their future.

Lifelong Learning: Cultivating Skills for a Dynamic World

Education does not end with graduation. In alignment with Finland's approach to lifelong learning, the School of Tomorrow will provide ongoing education opportunities for individuals of all ages, from recent graduates to mid-career professionals (Sahlberg, 2015). Community learning centers, online courses, and flexible certification programs will enable adults to continue building their skills and knowledge, adapting to the changing demands of the workforce.

Through partnerships with community organizations and local businesses, adults can access skill-building programs in fields ranging from advanced technology to creative arts. This commitment to lifelong learning not only prepares individuals for career shifts but fosters a culture of continuous growth, adaptability, and innovation.

Conclusion: An Educational Evolution for a Global Future

The School of Tomorrow represents a transformative shift toward a holistic, adaptable, and student-centered education system. By combining the strengths of Master Teachers and Apprentice Teachers, rethinking assessment practices, creating dynamic learning environments, and integrating real-world experiences into the curriculum, this model prepares students for the complexities of a global, digital society.

Grounded in international best practices and backed by research, this reimagined structure challenges outdated paradigms and prioritizes learning outcomes that are both academically rigorous and practically relevant. This evolution of education aligns with the needs of a changing world, ensuring that every student has the opportunity to develop into a capable, confident, and adaptable learner.

CHAPTER 6
Master Teachers as Leaders of Transformation: Elevating Education Through Expertise and Innovation

"The mediocre teacher tells. The good teacher explains. The superior teacher demonstrates. The great teacher inspires." ~ William Arthur Ward.

In a world where education is the key to future success, the role of the teacher remains paramount. Research consistently shows that teachers are the most significant in-school factor influencing student learning outcomes, surpassing other school-related variables like curriculum or class size. The RAND Corporation's study reveals that teacher quality alone can account for up to 30% of the variability in student performance, meaning it is the quality of the teacher's instructional ability that determines the level of academic success of students. This underscores a skilled, dedicated teacher's critical impact on a student's educational journey and future potential. This profound influence emphasizes the need for a reimagined education system that places Master Teachers—exceptional educators with advanced training, specialized knowledge, and leadership skills—at the forefront. These Master Teachers would serve as respected leaders, mentors, and supervisors, fostering student growth and future educators' development. This approach honors the teacher's pivotal role and ensures that students receive consistent, high-quality instruction that can transform their learning experiences and life outcomes. A talented teacher with outstanding instructional talent can replace the hope prevalent in our current system with irrefutable certainty towards students' success.

This chapter outlines a vision for an educational future led by Master Teachers—a select group of educators who teach and shape the profession by leading training, writing rigorous curricula, developing daily lesson plans, and serving as evaluators for their apprentices. These Master Teachers will embody the highest standards of professionalism and instructional expertise, transforming how schools function and students learn.

Unified School Scheduling: Empowering Master Teachers to Lead Across Districts

In practice, maximizing the impact of Master Teachers involves synchronizing school schedules across the district to enable seamless, large-scale virtual teaching. With a unified schedule, Master Teachers can leverage advanced technology to deliver instruction simultaneously to classrooms across different schools, effectively "beaming" into each classroom in real-time. For example, in a district where every secondary school follows the same bell schedule, Master Teachers can present live lessons, engage in discussions, and answer questions with students from multiple locations at once, using interactive video technology and digital learning platforms to facilitate active participation. This model increases the reach of highly qualified teachers and ensures that students across the district receive consistent, high-quality instruction regardless of their school's location or resources (Schleicher, 2018).

Such an approach allows for a more equitable distribution of top-tier teaching talent, particularly benefiting students in under-resourced schools who may not otherwise have access to highly skilled educators. Additionally, on-site Apprentice Teachers and classroom assistants provide direct support, ensuring students remain engaged and maintaining classroom management. This team-based model allows Master Teachers to concentrate on delivering content-rich lessons while apprentices and assistants manage individual and small-group support, reinforcing and extending learning as needed. Research from the OECD supports this approach, indicating that technology-enabled teaching models can reduce disparities in educational quality by extending the expertise of Master Teachers to a broader student base (OECD, 2022).

In this model, Teacher Apprentices—aspiring educators on track to becoming Master Teachers—will be physically present in the classrooms. Their role is critical to maintaining the integrity of the learning environment. Apprentices ensure academic integrity, uphold behavior norms, and maintain equity within the classroom while supporting students as they engage with the lesson remotely delivered by the Master Teacher. The apprentices act as facilitators, ensuring the students remain focused and engaged and receive the help they need to understand the material (Sahlberg, 2015) fully.

This partnership between technology and on-site support ensures that students benefit from the expertise of Master Teachers while still having the necessary in-person support to address individual needs. The combination of remote expert teaching and local guidance offers a highly effective and scalable solution to the teacher shortage problem while ensuring high-quality education for all students (OECD, 2022).

Master Teachers: The New Leaders in Education

Master Teachers are no longer confined to the traditional classroom role. Instead, they serve as leaders and supervisors responsible for shaping instructional practices across the district. These educators are not just experts in their subjects but skilled mentors who guide Teacher Apprentices through collaborative planning, curriculum creation, and activity and assessment design (Schleicher, 2018).

Master Teachers will also be instrumental in writing rigorous curricula that surpass state standards, pushing students to engage in deeper critical thinking and problem-solving. Their work will replace traditional grading systems with project-based assessments and portfolios, offering more meaningful evaluations of student progress and mastery. By focusing on real-world applications and evidence of learning, Master Teachers help students develop essential skills for success beyond the classroom (Sahlberg, 2015).

Furthermore, Master Teachers evaluate their apprentices, provide feedback, set goals, and ensure each apprentice is on track to become a highly skilled educator. This evaluation process ensures that the quality of education remains consistent and that apprentices continuously improve under the guidance of the Master Teachers (OECD, 2022).

Teacher Apprentices: Building the Next Generation of Educators

Teacher Apprentices are integral to sustaining this model of education. These aspiring educators work under the supervision of Master Teachers, gaining practical experience and developing their teaching skills. Unlike traditional student teachers, apprentices are not left to manage classrooms independently. Instead, they are part of a rigorous training process that prepares them for the complexities of teaching in a modern classroom (Sahlberg, 2015).

Apprentices participate actively in collaborative planning, curriculum design, and assessment creation alongside Master Teachers. They learn how to design lessons that align with academic standards while fostering creativity, adaptability, and critical thinking in students. In addition, apprentices assist with implementing project-based assessments, helping students work through real-world problems that allow them to demonstrate mastery over time (Schleicher, 2018).

This model creates a pipeline of skilled educators well-prepared to step into leadership roles as future Master Teachers. Through continuous evaluation and mentorship, apprentices are given the tools and support they need to grow and succeed in the profession (OECD, 2022).

Assessments and Student Progress: Project-Based Learning and Portfolios

In this reimagined system, traditional grading is replaced with project-based assessments and portfolios that showcase students' work and progress over time. Rather than relying on standardized tests or letter grades, students will complete projects that require them to apply their knowledge to real-world scenarios. These projects allow students to engage in deeper learning, foster creativity, and develop problem-solving skills (Sahlberg, 2015).

Portfolios will include various work products, such as essays, presentations, and projects, demonstrating students' ability to think critically, solve problems, and collaborate. Master Teachers will evaluate these portfolios, ensuring students meet high standards of excellence before progressing to the next level (Schleicher, 2018).

Portfolios in this reimagined education model will serve as comprehensive, reflective records of student growth, showcasing a wide range of work products—including essays, presentations, projects, and collaborative assignments—that illustrate students' critical thinking, problem-solving abilities, and collaborative skills. Each portfolio will be graded holistically by Master Teachers, who will assess not only the final products but also the learning process, creativity, and application of skills. This approach moves away from traditional letter grades. It emphasizes mastery, providing students with detailed feedback on their strengths and areas for improvement rather than reducing their efforts to a single final grade (Schleicher, 2018).

Internationally, countries like Finland and New Zealand have pioneered using portfolios as part of their assessment systems, allowing students to demonstrate learning across multiple competencies without relying solely on exams. In Finland, students compile portfolios focusing on creativity, problem-solving, and real-world applications, which teachers review and contribute to overall performance assessments. The Buck Institute for Education has shown that portfolio-based assessments rooted in project-based learning (PBL) deepen students' critical thinking, improve knowledge retention, and encourage a more robust engagement with material. By incorporating PBL, students are encouraged to apply skills that reflect real-world tasks, thus promoting meaningful ownership of their learning process.

Under this system, students advance based on demonstrated

proficiency rather than traditional grades, aligning with research that suggests students thrive in environments prioritizing mastery over numerical or letter grades (OECD, 2022). This method supports personalized learning paths, with students working towards clear, rigorous standards by Master Teachers trained to evaluate portfolios for depth, creativity, and problem-solving. By integrating detailed feedback and constructive critiques, this portfolio system provides a nuanced and supportive framework for student growth and academic development, helping them cultivate the skills necessary for future success.

Ensuring Funding Equity: Petitioning States for Support

With fewer teachers in this more efficient model, some states might reduce funding based on outdated formulas focusing on teacher-student ratios. To prevent this, school districts must petition states for equal or increased reimbursement, ensuring that districts maintain adequate funding despite fewer teachers. This funding is crucial to supporting the high salaries of Master Teachers, providing cutting-edge technology for remote instruction, and investing in the professional development of Teacher Apprentices (Schleicher, 2018).

Policymakers must recognize that although fewer teachers are employed, the quality of instruction will be vastly improved, and the overall demands on the district will remain substantial. By ensuring that funding levels remain consistent or even increase, districts can successfully implement this innovative model without sacrificing student resources (OECD, 2022).

A New Vision for Schools: Excellence as the Standard

This new educational model challenges us to rethink how schools and districts function. Master Teachers are instructional practice leaders, guiding Teacher Apprentices and shaping the learning environment. This mentorship and collaboration elevate the teaching profession and ensure students receive the highest quality education possible

(Schleicher, 2018).

The restructuring of traditional grades into project-based assessments and portfolios ensures that students are evaluated based on their true capabilities, not just their ability to memorize facts or perform on standardized tests. This approach fosters deeper engagement and learning, equipping students with the skills they need to navigate an increasingly complex world (Sahlberg, 2015).

By addressing funding challenges at the state level and ensuring that districts receive adequate support, we create a system where innovation is supported, not penalized. This visionary model allows students and teachers to thrive, building an education system that prioritizes excellence over mediocrity and prepares everyone involved for success in the 21st century (OECD, 2022).

Conclusion: Leading the Future of Education

Master Teachers will stand at the forefront of this educational revolution—leaders, mentors, and innovators who guide the next generation of educators and students alike. Through their expertise, dedication, and vision, we will build an education system that prioritizes quality over quantity, excellence over mediocrity, and learning over testing (Schleicher, 2018).

We embrace project-based assessments, portfolios, and the apprenticeship model to create an environment where students and teachers can thrive. This is not simply a reform of the current system—it is a complete reinvention of education as we know it. With Master Teachers leading the way, we will create schools that are genuinely prepared to meet the challenges of the 21st century, equip students with the skills they need to succeed, and ensure that the teaching profession remains a respected and essential pillar of our society.

CHAPTER 7
FROM SPECTATORS TO ARCHITECTS: REDEFINING LEADERSHIP IN TOMORROW'S SCHOOLS

As we envision the future of education, we must also reimagine the role of school leadership. Transforming schools into dynamic, student-centered learning environments requires a parallel evolution in how we approach leadership. In the School of Tomorrow, leaders are no longer passive managers overwhelmed by bureaucratic tasks and compliance. Instead, they are architects of learning, fully engaged in shaping instruction, fostering teacher growth, and creating the conditions for student success (Schleicher, 2018).

The focus shifts from management to engagement, as leaders take an active role in the instructional process, supporting teachers, guiding apprentices, and ensuring that every aspect of the school is aligned with the vision of preparing students for a rapidly changing world. This chapter explores how the future school model shapes the responsibilities and actions of school leaders, down to their daily interactions with staff and students.

Leadership in the School of Tomorrow: From Compliance to Engagement

In the School of Tomorrow, the traditional role of the principal or school administrator is fundamentally redefined. Rather than being bogged down by paperwork, compliance, and operational duties, school leaders now act as instructional architects who help design, implement, and sustain the school's educational vision (OECD, 2022).

The new model requires leaders to deeply understand pedagogy, technological integration, and students' developmental needs. Their role is to foster an environment where Master Teachers and Apprentices can thrive and where students constantly engage in experiential, project-based learning geared towards real-world applications. Leaders support this environment by being present in classrooms, guiding instruction, and providing timely, constructive feedback to teachers (Sahlberg, 2015).

To achieve this, leadership roles are divided into two key components: Coaching Days and Office Days. This balance allows leaders to fulfill their operational duties without losing focus on their primary responsibility—supporting teaching and learning (Schleicher, 2018).

Coaching Days: Architects of Learning

On Coaching Days, school leaders immerse themselves in the instructional process, conducting continuous learning walkthroughs, coaching teachers, and collaborating with instructional support staff. These walkthroughs are structured yet flexible, allowing leaders to observe classroom dynamics and identify trends that align with the school's improvement goals. Leaders focus on student engagement, differentiation, and the effectiveness of project-based learning, collecting evidence that can be used to enhance instruction across the school (OECD, 2022).

The observations during these walkthroughs are non-evaluative and aimed at fostering growth rather than judgment. After completing their classroom visits, leaders engage teachers in collaborative debriefing sessions, discussing observations and offering insights on refining and improving instructional practices. These peer-focused conversations encourage a shared learning experience where leaders and teachers reflect on what is working and what needs to change (Schleicher, 2018).

Additionally, leaders take time to coach Apprentice Teachers, helping them develop the skills they need to become Master Teachers. These sessions focus on classroom management, instructional design, and differentiated instruction, ensuring that Apprentices receive the mentorship and guidance necessary to master their craft (Sahlberg, 2015).

Triangulating Findings and Targeted Professional Development

After Coaching Days, administrators and instructional support staff collaborate to triangulate findings from their walkthroughs and teacher feedback sessions. This joint effort involves data analysis to identify instructional trends, areas for improvement, and successes that can be shared across the school. By pooling their observations, leaders comprehensively understand the school's instructional landscape and can plan targeted interventions to address any identified gaps (OECD, 2022).

This data informs professional development sessions tailored to the specific needs of the school's teachers. For example, if walkthrough data suggests that students are struggling with critical thinking tasks, the leadership team may organize a workshop focused on strategies for teaching higher-order thinking skills. These responsive, professional development sessions ensure teachers receive timely support directly tied to their practice (Schleicher, 2018).

Using data from walkthroughs and teacher feedback, school leaders ensure that professional development is not a generic, one-size-fits-all approach but customized to meet the school's unique needs. This targeted support helps teachers continuously refine their practice, leading to improved student outcomes (Sahlberg, 2015).

Office Days: Efficiency and Support Behind the Scenes

While Coaching Days allow leaders to engage directly with instruction, Office Days are dedicated to managing the operational responsibilities that keep the school running smoothly. Leaders use this time to handle administrative tasks such as budgeting, scheduling, compliance with state and federal regulations, and resource allocation. However, even on

Office Days, the focus remains on how these operational tasks support the educational vision (OECD, 2022).

Leaders collaborate with district administrators to ensure that resources are allocated effectively, aligning budgets with instructional priorities and the needs of teachers and students. By designating specific times for these tasks, leaders can manage the demands of running a school without letting operational duties overshadow their role as instructional leaders (Schleicher, 2018).

The Role of Instructional Support: Enhancing Classroom Innovation

Instructional support staff, including Instructional Coaches, Curriculum Specialists, and technology integration experts, play a pivotal role in this new model. They work alongside school leaders to support teachers and apprentices in implementing innovative instructional practices. On Coaching Days, instructional support staff participate in walkthroughs, provide targeted coaching, and collaborate on professional development efforts.

Their primary goal is to enhance classroom innovation, ensuring teachers have the tools and strategies to engage students in project-based learning, critical thinking, and real-world problem-solving. They serve as a bridge between the school's instructional goals and the classroom, helping to translate the educational vision into actionable teaching practices (OECD, 2022).

By working closely with school leaders and teachers, instructional support staff help create a cohesive instructional strategy that promotes classroom consistency while allowing for the flexibility needed to meet individual student needs. Their role is essential in ensuring the Master Teacher and Apprentice Model is effectively implemented and sustained (Schleicher, 2018).

Supporting Equity and Excellence: Leaders as Champions of Change

In this new educational structure, school leaders are champions of equity and excellence. Their role extends beyond the school's walls, including building partnerships with local businesses, industries, and community organizations. These partnerships help create pathways to success for students, whether enrolling in college, entering the workforce, or starting their businesses. Leaders work closely with district administrators and external partners to establish state-approved pathways that provide students with real-world learning opportunities and career readiness (Sahlberg, 2015).

Leaders also play a crucial role in ensuring that equity is at the forefront of every decision. This includes advocating for resources, supporting diverse learners, and ensuring every student can access high-quality instruction, regardless of background or circumstances. Leaders must actively address any barriers to success related to socioeconomic status, race, or learning differences (OECD, 2022).

Building a Culture of Continuous Improvement

The School of Tomorrow's leadership model is built on continuous improvement. Leaders are responsible for fostering growth in teachers and students and constantly evaluating and refining their practices. This reflective approach ensures that leadership remains dynamic and responsive to the changing needs of the school community (Schleicher, 2018).

By shifting from passive management to active engagement, school leaders help build a culture where learning and improvement are valued at every level—from students to teachers to leaders. This culture fosters an environment where innovation thrives, challenges are met with creative solutions, and every school community member is empowered to succeed (OECD, 2022).

Conclusion: Leadership for the 21st-Century School

The redefined role of school leaders in the School of Tomorrow represents a fundamental shift in how we approach educational leadership. No longer spectators, leaders become architects of learning, deeply involved in shaping the instructional environment and fostering teacher growth. Through a balance of Coaching Days and Office Days, leaders can engage in both their schools' operational and instructional aspects, ensuring that every decision is aligned with the school's vision for student success (Schleicher, 2018).

Leaders create schools where equity and excellence are the norm by supporting teachers, guiding apprentices, and building partnerships. Their commitment to continuous improvement ensures that the school remains at the forefront of educational innovation, preparing students for the challenges and opportunities of the 21st century (Sahlberg, 2015).

With this new vision for leadership, we can transform our schools into dynamic learning environments that truly meet the needs of all students, fostering their ability to succeed in a rapidly changing world (OECD, 2022).

CHAPTER 8
INSTRUCTIONAL SUPPORT IN THE SCHOOL OF TOMORROW: EMPOWERING TEACHERS AND ENHANCING STUDENT OUTCOMES

"IF WE TEACH TODAY'S STUDENTS AS WE TAUGHT YESTERDAY'S, WE ROB THEM OF TOMORROW." ~ JOHN DEWEY

As education transforms, the role of instructional support—including Instructional Coaches, Curriculum Specialists, and district staff—becomes more critical than ever. In the School of Tomorrow, instructional support is pivotal in ensuring that Master Teachers, Apprentice Teachers, and students thrive within a system designed to foster collaborative learning, innovative teaching, and real-world readiness.

Instructional support staff are the backbone of educational innovation, providing teachers with the guidance, resources, and professional development they need to succeed. These professionals are essential to creating a cohesive instructional strategy, bridging the gap between district goals and classroom practice, and ensuring the entire educational community works toward a shared vision.

This chapter delves into the vital role of instructional support within the Master Teacher and Apprentice Model. It explores how these individuals help to shape the future of education by driving instructional improvement, promoting professional growth, and ensuring equitable outcomes for all students.

Instructional Coaches: Guiding Teacher Growth and Practice

Instructional Coaches are at the heart of professional development in the School of Tomorrow. They work directly with Master and Apprentice Teachers to help refine their instructional practices, integrate new teaching methods, and ensure that student-centered learning remains at the forefront of classroom activities. Instructional Coaches provide personalized support, offer feedback, model lessons, and help teachers implement project-based learning and other innovative strategies.

Collaborative Professional Development

Coaches are crucial in organizing collaborative professional development sessions, where teachers share best practices, troubleshoot challenges, and co-create lessons that align with the school's instructional goals. These data-driven sessions are informed by real-time classroom observations, student performance data, and insights gathered during Coaching Days.

The role of Instructional Coaches is not limited to delivering content-specific training; they also focus on pedagogical development—helping teachers improve their skills in areas such as differentiation, classroom management, and technology integration. By offering targeted coaching based on each teacher's needs, Instructional Coaches ensure that all educators—whether they are Master Teachers or Apprentice Teachers—are constantly improving their practice.

Supporting New Teachers

Apprentice Teachers, in particular, benefit greatly from the support of Instructional Coaches. As these teachers work toward certification and mastery, they require ongoing mentorship and feedback. Instructional Coaches collaborate closely with Apprentice Teachers, helping them navigate the complexities of teaching while providing them with the tools they need to eventually take on the responsibilities of Master Teachers. This mentorship accelerates the professional growth of Apprentice Teachers, ensuring that they are well-prepared to lead classrooms independently in the future.

Instructional Coaches help foster a culture of continuous improvement within the school, ensuring that every teacher, regardless of experience level, has the support and resources they need to succeed.

Curriculum Specialists: Innovating Instructional Design

While Instructional Coaches focus on implementing teaching strategies, Curriculum Specialists are responsible for designing and aligning curricula with the school's educational vision. In the School of Tomorrow, Curriculum Specialists ensure students engage with rigorous, relevant content that incorporates real-world applications and prepares them for future challenges.

Designing Project-Based Learning

One of the critical responsibilities of Curriculum Specialists is to design and refine project-based learning units that encourage students to apply their knowledge in meaningful ways. This approach requires careful planning, alignment with state standards, and close collaboration with Master Teachers to ensure the projects are challenging and engaging for students.

Curriculum Specialists work with teachers to create interdisciplinary projects that connect subjects like math, science, history, and language arts to real-world issues. For example, students might work on a project that addresses environmental sustainability, requiring them to research, analyze data, and propose solutions—all while honing their skills in various academic disciplines. These projects are designed to foster critical thinking, collaboration, and problem-solving—skills essential for success in the modern world.

Aligning Assessments with Learning Goals

Authentic assessments in this model involve students engaging in tasks that mirror real-life challenges, requiring them to apply knowledge and skills in meaningful, practical ways. For example, a science assessment might ask students to design a sustainable ecosystem model. At the same time, a history project might involve creating a museum exhibit on a particular era, demonstrating both research and storytelling abilities. Curriculum Specialists work alongside Master and Apprentice Teachers to ensure these assessments measure critical thinking, problem-solving, and collaborative skills rather than rote memorization. This approach aligns with the Buck Institute for Education research, which supports the benefits of project-based learning (PBL) in deepening understanding and improving knowledge retention. Students gain experience in handling complex, multifaceted tasks by focusing on authentic assessments, preparing them for real-world applications and future success.

By aligning assessments with learning goals, Curriculum Specialists ensure student progress is measured meaningfully, reflecting their overall growth. These assessments are often integrated into student portfolios, which provide a comprehensive view of a student's development over time.

District Staff: Aligning Resources and Vision

While Instructional Coaches and Curriculum Specialists work directly with teachers and students, district staff play a broader role in ensuring that the resources and policies needed to support the Master Teacher and Apprentice Model are in place. District staff are responsible for resource allocation and ensuring that schools have the technology, professional development opportunities, and materials required to implement innovative instructional practices effectively.

Resource Allocation and Technology Integration

District staff work closely with school leaders to ensure that resources are allocated equitably across schools. This includes providing schools with the technology infrastructure to support virtual instruction, digital learning zones, and flexible classroom environments. They also play a critical role in securing funding for ongoing professional development and technology upgrades, ensuring that Master and Apprentice Teachers have the tools they need to succeed.

By working with school boards and state education agencies, district staff advocates for revised funding formulas that reflect the realities of the School of Tomorrow, where fewer teachers may be employed. However, the quality of instruction is significantly enhanced. Their role in budget management and policy advocacy ensures that schools are adequately supported in implementing this innovative model.

Ensuring Equity and Access

Another critical responsibility of district staff is to ensure that equity and access are at the heart of all district policies and initiatives. This includes ensuring that under-resourced schools receive the support they need to provide students with the same high-quality education in more affluent areas. District staff works to close the opportunity gap by providing targeted funding and resources to schools that serve economically disadvantaged communities.

District staff also ensure that instructional support is distributed equitably, with Coaches and Curriculum Specialists deployed to schools based on need. By focusing on equity, district staff help ensure that all students—regardless of their background—have access to the tools and opportunities they need to succeed.

Fostering a Culture of Collaboration and Growth

The success of the School of Tomorrow hinges on collaboration between instructional support staff, teachers, and school leaders. Instructional Coaches, Curriculum Specialists, and district staff all play complementary roles in creating a system that supports continuous improvement and innovation.

Regular triangulation meetings between these groups ensure that classroom data-driven insights are shared and used to inform instructional strategies. These meetings allow ongoing reflection on what is working and needs to be adjusted, creating a feedback loop that promotes growth at every school system level.

By fostering a culture of collaboration and growth, instructional support staff help create an environment where teachers feel empowered to take risks, innovate, and constantly refine their practice.

This culture ensures that students receive the highest quality education possible and that teachers remain motivated and supported throughout their careers.

Conclusion: Instructional Support as the Key to Success

Instructional support staff are the unsung heroes of the School of Tomorrow. They work behind the scenes to ensure that every teacher and student is set up for success. Through coaching, curriculum design, resource allocation, and policy advocacy, these professionals ensure that the school's instructional vision is realized in every classroom.

By supporting teachers in their professional growth and providing the resources needed to implement innovative teaching practices, instructional support staff help create schools where learning is meaningful, engagement is high, and success is within reach for every student. Their role is indispensable in building an education system that is equitable, effective, and sustainable for the 21st century.

In the School of Tomorrow, instructional support staff are not just facilitators—they are architects of success, ensuring that every aspect of teaching and learning is aligned to prepare students for a rapidly changing world. Through their dedication and expertise, they help create schools where excellence is the standard and every student has the opportunity to reach their full potential.

CHAPTER 9
TRANSFORMING CLASSROOM DESIGN FOR THE 21ST CENTURY

"THE BEST WAY TO PREDICT THE FUTURE IS TO CREATE IT." ~ PETER DRUCKER

The traditional classroom, with its rows of desks facing a single teacher at the front of the room, is a relic of the past. As we move toward a future where collaboration, creativity, and critical thinking are paramount, we must radically rethink how classrooms are designed. The School of Tomorrow demands spaces that are not only adaptable to various learning styles but also equipped with the technology and tools necessary to prepare students for an increasingly complex and connected world. This chapter explores how innovative classroom design will foster a new kind of learning, where students are active participants in their education, and the classroom becomes a living laboratory for exploration, discovery, and growth (Schleicher, 2018).

The Flexible Classroom: A Space for Collaboration and Creativity

In the School of Tomorrow, classrooms are no longer static environments where students passively receive information. Instead, they are flexible, dynamic spaces that can be rearranged to support various learning activities— from independent work to group projects and hands-on experimentation. The key to this flexibility lies in using modular furniture and adaptable layouts. Chairs on wheels, mobile tables, and lounge-style seating allow students to shift quickly between collaborative work, individual reflection, and teacher-led instruction (OECD, 2022).

In Finland, classrooms are designed to offer flexibility and support student autonomy, encouraging learners to take charge of their education. Finnish classrooms often use open-plan layouts that include distinct activity zones, each tailored to specific tasks. For instance, a quiet zone for reading and individual work might be equipped with comfortable seating and minimal distractions. Another area could be set up for collaborative projects, featuring group tables and interactive tools like whiteboards or digital displays. Additionally, hands-on or experimental learning zones allow students to engage in practical tasks, such as science experiments or art projects, with the necessary resources and space for creativity and exploration.

This arrangement allows students to select the zone that best matches their task, whether working independently, brainstorming with peers, or engaging in hands-on activities. The design fosters independence and self-directed learning, as students are empowered to determine their learning environment based on their needs and preferences (Sahlberg, 2015). This model is becoming more influential internationally, as countries explore how flexible learning environments contribute to engagement, critical thinking, and a sense of ownership over learning (OECD, 2022).

In the School of Tomorrow, each classroom is divided into distinct learning zones that can be customized based on the lesson's needs. These zones include collaborative stations for group work, quiet zones for independent study, and maker spaces where students can engage in hands-on projects. These adaptable environments foster creativity and critical thinking, encouraging students to take ownership of their learning and collaborate with their peers to solve complex problems (Schleicher, 2018).

Technology-Integrated Learning Zones: Bridging the Physical and Digital Worlds

Technology is the backbone of the modern classroom, enabling students to access information, connect with experts, and collaborate with peers worldwide. Technology is fully integrated into the learning environment in the School of Tomorrow, blurring the lines between the physical and digital worlds (OECD, 2022).

Interactive screens, augmented reality (AR), and virtual reality (VR) tools allow students to explore new concepts in immersive ways. For example, students studying ancient history could use VR headsets to virtually visit the ruins of ancient civilizations, experiencing them as if they were there. In Singapore, where education is heavily focused on innovation, schools have begun integrating VR and AR into science and geography lessons, allowing students to visualize complex processes and explore virtual environments in real time (Schleicher, 2018).

Classrooms have digital learning stations where students can engage with interactive software, complete virtual labs, or work on coding projects. These stations are designed to support individual learning and collaborative tasks, ensuring that students of all abilities can engage meaningfully with the content. AI-driven learning platforms personalize the learning experience for each student, providing real-time feedback and tailored support based on their progress (OECD, 2022).

Furthermore, technology-integrated classrooms in the School of Tomorrow are equipped with smart boards, digital whiteboards, and collaborative screens, where students can share their work with the class, receive instant feedback, and collectively problem-solve. The seamless integration of technology into every learning experience enhances student engagement, deepens understanding, and prepares students for a future where digital literacy is essential (Sahlberg, 2015).

The Global Classroom: Connecting Students Across Borders

One of the most exciting innovations in the School of Tomorrow is the global classroom, where students collaborate with peers worldwide in real-time. Through video conferencing, shared digital workspaces, and global project-based learning, students gain a broader perspective on global issues while developing cross-cultural communication and teamwork skills (OECD, 2022).

In countries like Estonia, known for its digital-first education system, schools embrace global connectivity by partnering with classrooms in other countries for joint projects. Estonian students work with peers in countries like Japan, Germany, and Finland on environmental science projects, coding challenges, and collaborative research. These partnerships expose students to different perspectives and help them develop a global mindset that will be invaluable in their future careers (Schleicher, 2018).

In the School of Tomorrow, every classroom is connected to a global network of learners. Students can work together on shared challenges such as climate change, global health, or sustainable development, leveraging the expertise of their peers from different parts of the world. This global collaboration enriches the learning experience by introducing students to diverse ideas, cultures, and ways of thinking, fostering empathy and cultural awareness (Sahlberg, 2015).

Sustainability and Innovation: Designing Schools for the Future

The physical design of schools in the School of Tomorrow also reflects a commitment to sustainability and innovation. School buildings are designed to be energy-efficient, incorporating features such as solar panels, green roofs, and rainwater harvesting systems. These sustainable features are good for the environment and serve as learning tools for students, who can study how renewable energy systems work, monitor their school's energy consumption, and develop solutions for reducing waste (OECD, 2022).

Incorporating biophilic design—an approach that integrates natural elements like plants, natural light, and outdoor learning spaces—transforms the learning environment into a setting that supports students' physical and mental well-being. Biophilic design goes beyond simply adding greenery; it creates an immersive experience where students interact with nature daily. For instance, classrooms might feature large windows that allow ample natural light, indoor plants that improve air quality, and textures inspired by the natural world. Outdoor classrooms and gardens, which Denmark and Japan have successfully implemented, enable students to engage in hands-on learning activities, like science experiments or art projects, surrounded by nature.

Students benefit from this exposure to natural elements in numerous ways. Research shows that biophilic design reduces stress, improves focus, and enhances cognitive function, positively impacting learning outcomes (Schleicher, 2018). Studies indicate that access to nature boosts creativity and encourages open-minded problem-solving as students become more engaged and curious in a space that feels both stimulating and relaxing. Incorporating biophilic principles in education also supports sustainable values, fostering an appreciation for the environment and encouraging students to develop a lifelong connection to the natural world (OECD, 2022).

The School of Tomorrow is designed to be modular, allowing spaces to be easily reconfigured as the needs of the school and its students evolve. Classrooms can be expanded or contracted, walls can be moved, and learning zones can be adapted to accommodate new technologies and teaching methods. This level of flexibility ensures that the physical environment remains future-proof, capable of supporting new educational innovations as they arise (Sahlberg, 2015).

Learning Beyond the Classroom: Experiential Education

In the School of Tomorrow, learning is not confined to the four walls of the classroom. Experiential education is at the heart of the learning experience, with students regularly participating in field trips, service-learning projects, and internships that connect their studies to the real world (Schleicher, 2018).

Countries like Finland and New Zealand have long integrated "learning by doing" into their national curricula, recognizing the profound benefits of experiential, hands-on education. For instance, a typical school day in Finland might include an outing to a nearby forest, where students participate in ecosystem studies. They observe local plant and animal species, engage in soil and water testing, and discuss biodiversity and environmental impact. These activities provide students with a tangible understanding of ecological concepts and reinforce critical thinking as they analyze data gathered from the field (Sahlberg, 2015).

Similarly, students in New Zealand regularly engage in outdoor projects that bridge classroom learning with real-world applications. For example, primary students might participate in a "river study" program where they examine water quality, observe native aquatic life, and understand human impacts on their environment. This hands-on experience enhances their science skills and fosters a sense of responsibility toward environmental stewardship. By immersing students in nature and providing authentic learning contexts, these countries effectively cultivate critical thinking, problem-solving, and a deep respect for the natural world (OECD, 2022).

The School of Tomorrow expands on these concepts by ensuring every student can participate in experiential learning through partnerships with local businesses, internships in high-demand industries, or projects that address real-world challenges. These experiences help students develop critical thinking, problem-solving, and leadership skills while giving them a deeper understanding of the world (OECD, 2022).

Conclusion: The Future of Classroom Design

The School of Tomorrow represents a dramatic shift from the traditional classroom model. It is where flexibility, technology, and sustainability come together to create an environment that fosters collaboration, creativity, and critical thinking. By integrating global perspectives, technology-driven learning zones, and hands-on, experiential education, the School of Tomorrow prepares students for the challenges and opportunities of the 21st century (Schleicher, 2018).

As we look to the future, it is clear that the physical design of our schools will play a crucial role in shaping the educational experiences of our students. By creating adaptable, connected, and future-focused spaces, we can ensure that every student can thrive in an environment that supports their growth as learners and global citizens. The future of education begins with the classrooms we design today.

CHAPTER 10
EMBRACING TECHNOLOGY: ENHANCING LEARNING WITH MODERN TOOLS

"TECHNOLOGY WILL NEVER REPLACE GREAT TEACHERS, BUT TECHNOLOGY IN THE HANDS OF GREAT TEACHERS IS TRANSFORMATIONAL." ~ GEORGE COUROS

In the School of Tomorrow, technology is not an add-on or supplementary tool; it is an integral part of the learning experience, designed to enhance instruction, personalize education, and connect students with the world. This chapter explores how the seamless integration of cutting-edge technologies—from artificial intelligence to augmented reality—will redefine how we think about teaching and learning. By embracing technology, we can create equitable access to high-quality education, foster global collaboration, and prepare students for a future where digital literacy is as essential as traditional literacy (Schleicher, 2018).

AI-Driven Personalized Learning: Tailoring Education for Every Student

In the School of Tomorrow, artificial intelligence (AI) plays a central role in personalizing the learning experience for every student. AI-driven platforms analyze student performance, learning preferences, and engagement data to tailor instruction to each individual's needs. These platforms create personalized learning paths, offering real-time feedback, recommendations for additional resources, and adaptive assessments that adjust to the student's level of understanding (OECD, 2022).

Incorporating AI into the classroom allows teachers to move away from the traditional one-size-fits-all approach to education. Instead, each student can progress at their own pace, mastering content before moving on to more challenging material. This personalized approach helps bridge the gap between students who may struggle with certain concepts and those who are ready to accelerate their learning (Schleicher, 2018).

Countries like China and South Korea have already begun experimenting with AI in education, using it to identify students' strengths and weaknesses and provide targeted interventions. In China, AI systems track students' facial expressions during lessons to gauge their understanding and adjust the difficulty level of the content accordingly (Sahlberg, 2015). By harnessing the power of AI, the School of Tomorrow ensures that every student receives the support they need to succeed, regardless of their starting point.

Virtual Reality and Augmented Reality: Immersive Learning Experiences

Virtual reality (VR) and augmented reality (AR) can revolutionize the way students learn by creating immersive environments where they can explore concepts in previously unimaginable ways. In the School of Tomorrow, these technologies will be commonplace, allowing students to step inside the subjects they are studying (OECD, 2022).

Imagine a history lesson in which students don VR headsets and find themselves in ancient Rome, walking through the streets, interacting with historical figures, and witnessing key events as they unfold. Or a biology class in which AR overlays digital information onto real-world objects, allowing students to examine the inner workings of cells or explore the human body in intricate detail. These immersive experiences deepen understanding and make abstract concepts tangible (Schleicher, 2018).

Countries like Japan are already incorporating VR and AR into classrooms, particularly in subjects like science, where students can conduct virtual experiments that would be too dangerous or complex to perform in a physical lab (Sahlberg, 2015). In the School of Tomorrow, these technologies will be used not just for science and history but across all subjects, from virtual art galleries where students can create and manipulate 3D sculptures to interactive language lessons where they can practice speaking with AI-powered avatars (OECD, 2022).

Using VR and AR also opens up new opportunities for experiential learning. For instance, students could participate in virtual internships, gaining real-world experience in engineering, medicine, or architecture without leaving the classroom. These technologies provide students with hands-on learning opportunities, bridging the gap between theoretical knowledge and practical application (Schleicher, 2018).

Global Collaboration Through Technology: Breaking Down Geographic Barriers

One of the most transformative aspects of technology in education is its ability to connect students globally. In the School of Tomorrow, classrooms are not confined by geography; students regularly collaborate with their peers worldwide on projects that address global challenges such as climate change, public health, or sustainable development (OECD, 2022).

Using video conferencing platforms, cloud-based collaborative tools, and virtual project spaces, students can work together in real-time, regardless of where they are physically located. These global partnerships expose students to diverse perspectives, fostering a deeper understanding of global issues and developing their ability to work in cross-cultural teams (Schleicher, 2018). This collaboration is essential in preparing students for an increasingly interconnected world.

Estonia has successfully integrated global collaboration into its curriculum. Estonian students regularly work with their peers in other countries on joint projects, from coding challenges to environmental science initiatives (Sahlberg, 2015). This approach allows students to see the real-world impact of their studies and understand how they can contribute to solving global problems.

In the School of Tomorrow, global classrooms are a standard part of the curriculum, with students participating in virtual exchange programs, joint research projects, and international competitions. These experiences enhance students' academic skills and build empathy, cultural awareness, and the ability to collaborate across borders—skills vital for success in the 21st-century workforce (Schleicher, 2018).

The Role of Data and Analytics: Informed Decision-Making

Technology in the School of Tomorrow goes beyond enhancing the student experience; it also provides teachers and administrators with powerful tools for data analysis and decision-making. By collecting and analyzing data on student performance, engagement, and behavior, educators can make informed decisions about how to support their students best (OECD, 2022).

Learning management systems (LMS) and data dashboards provide real-time insights into student progress, allowing teachers to quickly identify those needing additional support or intervention. For example, if a student consistently struggles with a particular concept, the LMS can flag this for the teacher, who can provide targeted help. Similarly, if students excel in a particular area, the system can suggest enrichment opportunities to challenge them further (Schleicher, 2018).

In countries like Singapore, data analytics is already a crucial tool for personalizing learning and boosting educational outcomes. Schools use sophisticated data-tracking systems to monitor students' progress on a granular level, collecting information on everything from assessment scores to behavioral trends and engagement patterns. This data is analyzed to pinpoint areas where students may be struggling or excelling, allowing educators to tailor instructional strategies accordingly (Sahlberg, 2015). For example, if data reveals that a particular student is consistently scoring low in math, teachers can adjust the curriculum to include additional support, resources, or targeted interventions.

In the School of Tomorrow, data-driven approaches will be taken even further with AI-powered analytics and machine learning. Advanced systems will collect and analyze real-time data on student engagement, comprehension, and pace of learning, providing educators with instantaneous feedback on each student's progress. For instance, if AI detects that a group of students is struggling with a particular concept, it can recommend a more personalized set of resources or suggest small group sessions for focused review. Teachers equipped with these detailed insights can make immediate adjustments to instruction, optimizing their teaching strategies to better meet the needs of each learner (OECD, 2022).

Additionally, predictive analytics will help schools proactively address potential academic challenges by identifying patterns that indicate future learning obstacles. For example, suppose data reveals that students with lower attendance risk falling behind. In that case, schools can implement targeted support measures, such as mentorship programs or supplemental resources, to help those students stay on track. This continuous, data-informed feedback loop creates a dynamic and responsive educational environment, ensuring each student receives the tailored support necessary for success in real-time.

Ensuring Equity Through Technology: Bridging the Digital Divide

While technology can enhance education, it also presents challenges—particularly the risk of widening the digital divide between students with access to cutting-edge tools and those without. In the School of Tomorrow, ensuring equitable access to technology is a top priority (OECD, 2022).

To address the digital divide, schools will partner with governments, corporations, and non-profits to ensure every student has access to essential technology, such as devices and reliable internet, regardless of socio-economic status. Programs like ConnectED in the United States and Kenya's Digital Literacy Program offer compelling models. Launched in 2013, ConnectED focuses on expanding high-speed broadband access to under-resourced schools, providing students with devices like iPads, and training teachers to integrate technology effectively into the curriculum. ConnectED aims to bridge the digital divide by targeting underserved schools and empowering students to develop the tech skills needed in the modern world (U.S. Department of Education, 2020).

Similarly, Kenya's Digital Literacy Program (DLP), launched in 2016, equips primary school students with tablets, educational content, and teacher training to create technology-rich learning environments. This program is part of a national strategy to prepare students for a digital economy, with interactive literacy, numeracy, and science learning tools. The DLP has provided over one million devices to students and aims to integrate ICT skills into Kenya's education system, emphasizing digital competency as an essential component of future-ready education (Kenya Ministry of ICT, 2019).

Both programs demonstrate the transformative potential of such partnerships in closing technology access gaps, setting a standard for future initiatives that equip students with the digital resources required to succeed in an increasingly tech-driven world (Sahlberg, 2015).

In addition to providing the necessary hardware, schools will focus on digital literacy, ensuring that students can access technology and understand how to use it effectively. This includes teaching students how to navigate the internet safely, critically evaluate online information, and use digital tools to create, collaborate, and innovate (Schleicher, 2018).

By prioritizing equity, the School of Tomorrow ensures that all students, regardless of background, can benefit from technology's transformative power (OECD, 2022).

Building Digital Citizens: Preparing Students for a Connected World

In the School of Tomorrow, students are not just passive consumers of technology but digital citizens who understand how to use technology responsibly and ethically. As part of the curriculum, students will learn about cybersecurity, data privacy, digital etiquette, and the ethical implications of new technologies like AI and machine learning (Schleicher, 2018).

Programs in countries like Finland and Australia have already begun incorporating digital citizenship into their education systems, teaching students how to navigate the digital world safely and responsibly (Sahlberg, 2015). In the School of Tomorrow, this will be a core component of the curriculum, ensuring that students are not only technically proficient but also thoughtful and responsible users of technology (OECD, 2022).

This focus on digital citizenship prepares students for a future where they must navigate complex digital landscapes, understand the ethical implications of their actions, and contribute positively to the global digital community (Schleicher, 2018).

Conclusion: Embracing the Future with Technology

The School of Tomorrow is a place where technology is fully integrated into every aspect of the learning experience. The possibilities are endless, from AI-driven personalized learning to virtual reality field trips. By embracing these modern tools, we can create engaging, interactive, and equitable learning environments that prepare students for the future.

Technology can transform education, making it more personalized, collaborative, and connected than ever before. By embracing these innovations, we can ensure that every student has the opportunity to thrive in a world where digital literacy is essential and where global collaboration is the key to success.

The future is here, and it is digital. It is time to prepare our students to navigate and shape this new world (Schleicher, 2018).

CHAPTER 11
Parent and Community Engagement in the School of Tomorrow

"It takes a village to raise a child." ~ African Proverb

In the School of Tomorrow, the traditional roles of parents and communities in education are redefined to reflect the changing landscape of teaching and learning. Parents are no longer seen as mere participants in their child's education; they are partners. Communities are no longer viewed as external entities, disconnected from the daily workings of the school; they are integral to its success. This chapter explores how parental engagement and community partnerships can be transformed in the future, fostering an education system where collaboration between families, schools, and the broader community is essential to student success (Schleicher, 2018).

Parents as Partners: A Collaborative Approach

In the School of Tomorrow, parental engagement is redefined to enable meaningful contributions that actively support students' learning and development. Rather than limiting involvement to traditional roles like attending school events or assisting with homework, parents are integrated into the educational process in impactful ways. For example, parents may participate in learning workshops where they receive training on the curriculum and skills to support their child's learning at home. In the U.K., schools that involve parents through workshops and seminars see improved student performance, especially when parents reinforce literacy and numeracy skills at home (Goodall & Montgomery, 2014).

Additionally, parents in this model might join student-led conferences, a practice adopted in Sweden, where students present their work and progress to both teachers and parents. This format encourages students to take ownership of their learning while allowing parents to engage deeply in their child's academic journey. Moreover, community projects offer another avenue for involvement, where parents collaborate with schools on service-based learning initiatives. In Finland, for instance, community engagement is integral to the curriculum, with parents frequently involved in projects that teach civic responsibility and foster community ties (Sahlberg, 2015).

Finally, parents are also encouraged to participate in regular feedback loops with teachers, facilitated by digital platforms that keep them informed of their child's progress and challenges in real time. Such platforms, as used in Singapore, provide timely insights and open channels of communication, allowing parents to contribute meaningfully to goal-setting and monitor ongoing academic growth. Studies have shown that when parents are empowered to take on these expanded roles, student outcomes improve markedly, as they benefit from a cohesive support network that bridges school and home environments (OECD, 2022).

To ensure parents are equipped to be active partners, the School of Tomorrow provides ongoing training and resources that help parents understand the curriculum, learning objectives, and their role in reinforcing these lessons at home. This training is not merely informational; it is interactive and hands-on. Parents attend workshops on digital literacy, project-based learning, and social-emotional development, equipping them with the tools to support their children effectively (Sahlberg, 2015).

Communication between schools and parents is also more personalized and dynamic in this model. Teachers and school leaders use digital platforms to maintain real-time communication with parents, share student progress, offer suggestions for at-home reinforcement, and even collaborate on individual learning plans. This level of engagement ensures that parents are always aware of their child's progress and can actively guide their learning journey (Schleicher, 2018).

Student-led conferences replace traditional parent-teacher meetings, allowing students to demonstrate their learning and set goals with the input of both their teacher and parents. This collaborative approach empowers students, reinforces the importance of their agency in education, and helps parents understand their child's academic and personal development more comprehensively (OECD, 2022).

Empowering Families Through Flexibility and Choice

Families in the School of Tomorrow can choose learning environments that best suit their child's unique needs and interests. Parents work closely with educators to design personalized education plans that reflect their child's strengths, challenges, and aspirations. Schools offer flexible learning pathways, allowing students to pursue subjects they are passionate about while ensuring they meet core academic standards (Schleicher, 2018).

While students in the School of Tomorrow follow a curriculum grounded in core academic standards, families can create personalized pathways that cater to their child's individual strengths, challenges, and interests. Working closely with educators, parents co-design education plans that ensure foundational competencies in essential subjects like literacy, math, and science while also allowing space for students to dive deeply into areas of personal interest. This approach provides a balanced education that meets standardized requirements and nurtures students' unique skills and passions (Schleicher, 2018).

For example, a student interested in technology might spend part of their school day in a digital lab focused on coding and app development, gaining hands-on skills that connect directly to academic learning in math and logic. Meanwhile, a student passionate about environmental science might work on sustainability projects, collaborating with local conservation organizations to apply scientific concepts in real-world contexts. These individualized learning pathways maintain alignment with academic standards, ensuring students acquire foundational knowledge while engaging in meaningful, relevant projects that enhance their motivation and deepen their understanding (Sahlberg, 2015).

Schools also offer blended learning models, where students combine in-person and virtual learning. This flexibility allows students to balance schoolwork with other commitments, such as family responsibilities, extracurricular activities, or internships. Parents are deeply involved in designing these customized learning schedules, ensuring their child's education fits their family's unique lifestyle and needs (OECD, 2022).

This focus on choice and flexibility also extends to school selection. The School of Tomorrow embraces the idea that students should attend schools that match their interests and learning styles. This might involve magnet schools with specialized programs in areas like STEM, the arts, or entrepreneurship, or it could include partnerships with online learning platforms that allow students to take courses outside of their immediate district. This approach fosters a stronger connection between students, their families, and the schools they choose to attend, creating an educational ecosystem that works for everyone involved (Schleicher, 2018).

The Community as a Learning Laboratory

The concept of school as a siloed institution, separate from the broader community, no longer applies in the School of Tomorrow. Instead, schools and communities are deeply intertwined, with community resources and expertise woven into the fabric of the educational experience. Schools become innovation hubs, drawing on local businesses, non-profits, and cultural organizations to provide students with real-world learning experiences (OECD, 2022).

This integration starts with community partnerships. Schools work with local businesses, universities, and government agencies to develop career pathways that allow students to gain hands-on experience in various industries. These partnerships allow students to intern, shadow professionals, and work on real-life projects contributing to the local economy (Sahlberg, 2015).

For example, a high school student interested in engineering might partner with a local manufacturing company and work on a project that addresses a real-world engineering challenge. Another student passionate about public health might work with a local hospital or health department, participating in community health initiatives that make a tangible difference in their neighborhood. These experiences prepare students for future careers and help them understand their education's relevance to broader societal challenges (Schleicher, 2018).

Beyond the professional realm, community involvement extends to civic engagement. Students participate in service-learning projects, working on community development initiatives, such as building sustainable housing, organizing public art installations, or advocating for local policy changes. These projects are not merely add-ons to the curriculum but core components of the educational experience, helping students develop a sense of responsibility and connection to their communities (OECD, 2022).

The Schools of Tomorrow also function as community resource centers, offering spaces for community events, adult education courses, and public forums. This transforms the school into a lifelong learning hub, where education is not confined to K-12 students but extends to all community members. Schools become centers of civic engagement by offering programs that benefit the broader community, strengthening the relationship between schools and the neighborhoods they serve (Sahlberg, 2015).

Bridging Gaps Through Technology

Technology bridges the gap between schools, parents, and communities. The School of Tomorrow uses digital platforms to maintain constant communication between all stakeholders, ensuring that parents and community members are always connected to what is happening in the classroom (OECD, 2022).

For parents who may not be able to attend school events in person due to work or other commitments, schools offer virtual participation options, allowing them to attend parent-teacher conferences, school board meetings, and community events via video conferencing. These platforms also provide a space for community organizations to offer resources and opportunities to students, whether it is through virtual internships, online workshops, or digital career fairs (Schleicher, 2018).

Online portals give parents real-time access to their child's academic progress, behavioral reports, and upcoming assignments. Parents can communicate directly with teachers through these portals, ensuring they are always informed and involved in their child's education. These tools also help parents access learning resources to support their children at home, such as instructional videos, digital textbooks, and interactive learning games (Sahlberg, 2015).

Technology opens up new avenues for collaboration with schools for the broader community. Local businesses and non-profits can use digital platforms to connect with students for mentorship programs, guest lectures, or virtual tours of workplaces and facilities. These partnerships ensure that students can access various learning experiences, regardless of geographical or logistical constraints (OECD, 2022).

Creating a Supportive and Inclusive School Culture

In the School of Tomorrow, family and community engagement is not just about partnerships and participation but about creating a supportive and inclusive school culture where everyone feels valued and empowered to contribute. Schools focus on building trust and transparency in their relationships with parents and community members, ensuring that all voices are heard and respected (Schleicher, 2018).

One key strategy for fostering this culture is the development of family and community advisory councils, which include representatives from the school, parents, local businesses, and community organizations. These councils meet regularly to discuss school policies, share feedback, and collaborate on community-based initiatives. By involving parents and community members in decision-making processes, schools ensure that their policies reflect the needs and values of the broader community (Sahlberg, 2015).

In addition to advisory councils, schools host family and community engagement events, where parents and community members can come together to learn, share ideas, and celebrate student achievements. These events help build stronger relationships between families and schools, creating a more connected and supportive educational environment (OECD, 2022).

Schools also make a concerted effort to ensure that all families, regardless of socioeconomic background, feel welcome and supported. This includes offering language translation services, transportation assistance, and financial aid for participation in school activities. By removing barriers to engagement, schools can create a more inclusive environment where every family feels they are an essential part of their child's education (Schleicher, 2018).

Conclusion: A New Vision for Engagement

In the School of Tomorrow, parental and community engagement is not an afterthought but a core component of the educational process. By transforming schools into collaboration and community involvement hubs, we can create an education system responsive to students' needs, empowers families, and strengthens communities (OECD, 2022).

The future of education is one where parents and communities work hand-in-hand with schools to ensure every student has the support and resources they need to succeed. By embracing this vision of collaborative engagement, we can.

CHAPTER 12
Pathways to Success and Transformative Assessment

"The function of education is to teach one to think intensively and to think critically. Intelligence plus character—that is the goal of true education." ~ Martin Luther King Jr.

In an era defined by technological advancement and global interconnectedness, the School of Tomorrow strives to offer students more than traditional academic instruction. The dual focus on career readiness and transformative assessment practices equips students with the skills to navigate and excel in diverse future careers while fostering the adaptability to continue learning and growing in a dynamic world. This chapter delves into how these pathways and innovative assessment methods empower students to become active, engaged participants in their educational journeys and beyond.

Career Pathways: Creating Real-World Connections

The School of Tomorrow seeks to bridge the gap between education and workforce needs by developing clear, structured career pathways that begin early in students' schooling. Inspired by Germany's dual-education system, which combines classroom learning with in-field training, students are provided with real-world experiences that relate directly to their fields of interest. In Germany, this system effectively prepares students for roles in fields as diverse as finance, engineering, and healthcare by dividing their time between school-based instruction and hands-on apprenticeships. Adopting this approach, the School of Tomorrow offers similar experiences for students interested in technology, medicine, environmental science, and the arts.

For example, a student interested in environmental science might partner with local conservation groups to learn ecological restoration techniques and conduct fieldwork. Students interested in technology might collaborate with local companies, developing their coding and digital design skills in a real-world lab setting. Research from the Organization for Economic Co-operation and Development (OECD) shows that students involved in such applied learning pathways are more likely to gain meaningful employment upon graduation, as they graduate with both academic knowledge and practical, industry-relevant skills .

Lifelong Learning: The Finnish Model of Continuous Education

While the School of Tomorrow prepares students for specific career pathways, it also embraces the concept of lifelong learning, modeled on Finland's commitment to accessible, ongoing education for individuals of all ages. In Finland, education extends beyond childhood, providing adults with opportunities to adapt to workforce shifts and pursue personal interests. This commitment ensures that Finnish citizens are always able to learn new skills or transition to new career fields as needed, fostering a highly adaptable and resilient workforce.

Building on this model, the School of Tomorrow offers flexible learning options, such as night classes, weekend workshops, and online courses for recent graduates and adult learners. Courses cover topics ranging from technical certifications to personal development, allowing individuals at any stage of life to acquire the knowledge and competencies needed for their careers and personal growth. For example, a mid-career professional might enroll in a weekend coding boot camp offered by the school to gain digital skills for a career shift, while a recent graduate could take an evening course in leadership or management to prepare for advanced roles within their industry.

Integrating Technology: Learning Anytime, Anywhere

To make lifelong learning accessible, the School of Tomorrow relies heavily on technology, offering digital platforms where students can engage in both synchronous and asynchronous learning. Estonia's e-Estonia initiative provides a valuable model in this regard, where digital platforms are embedded at all levels of education, enabling students to access resources, track their progress, and engage in real-time feedback with teachers. Similarly, the School of Tomorrow's digital platforms provide students with a seamless, interactive, and customized learning experience, where they can log in to study modules, track their achievements, and access virtual classes taught by Master Teachers.

The advantages of integrating technology are particularly evident for students in remote areas, who can access the same high-quality education as those in urban centers. Moreover, digital learning platforms allow students to work at their own pace, a strategy that has been shown to improve retention rates and academic outcomes (OECD, 2022).

Transformative Assessment: Moving Beyond Standardized Testing

The School of Tomorrow's approach to assessment rejects the limitations of traditional standardized testing, favoring instead an assessment model that mirrors real-world problem-solving and critical thinking skills. In Finland, assessments are embedded in daily classroom activities rather than confined to high-stakes exams, focusing on formative feedback that helps students improve. The School of Tomorrow builds on this model by implementing project-based portfolios that evaluate students' ability to apply knowledge to practical challenges.

Portfolios may include a diverse range of work products, such as essays, lab reports, presentations, and collaborative projects, all reflecting students' competencies in core subjects and problem-solving. For example, a student interested in engineering might complete a capstone project involving designing and testing a bridge model, while a student focused on environmental science could create a report on a local ecosystem. Such projects, evaluated by Master Teachers, provide a comprehensive picture of students' skills and understanding, far beyond what traditional exams can capture.

Master Teachers: Leaders of Evaluation and Innovation

Master Teachers play a crucial role in this reimagined assessment model. As experts in their fields, they guide the development of assessments, mentor Apprentice Teachers, and set rigorous standards for student portfolios. Their expertise and advanced training ensure that students receive consistent, high-quality feedback on their work, supporting a cycle of continuous improvement. For instance, Master Teachers might review students' project portfolios, emphasizing creativity, collaboration, and critical thinking, and providing detailed feedback that students can use to refine their skills and understanding.

A study by the Buck Institute for Education has demonstrated that project-based learning enhances students' critical thinking abilities and improves their motivation and engagement. This approach makes assessment a learning tool rather than a barrier, encouraging students to actively participate in their educational growth.

Pathways to Career and Academic Success

Integrating career pathways and transformative assessments ultimately provides students with the technical skills and intellectual abilities required for success in the modern workforce. By partnering with industries, nonprofit organizations, and government agencies, the School of Tomorrow creates opportunities for students to gain professional experience before graduation. The Swiss VET program serves as an inspiration here, with its proven success in guiding students from academic settings directly into their chosen career fields, leading to high employment rates and a robust national workforce.

The School of Tomorrow's model ensures that each student's learning journey is aligned with their goals and interests, making education relevant, engaging, and purposeful. This approach does more than prepare students for specific jobs; it cultivates adaptable, resilient individuals equipped for lifelong learning in a rapidly changing world.

Conclusion

By combining a structured approach to career readiness with a transformative assessment model, the School of Tomorrow prepares students to become competent, reflective, and innovative members of society. Countries like Finland, Estonia, and Switzerland set examples that demonstrate the impact of aligning education with real-world applications, and the School of Tomorrow builds on these insights to create a future-ready educational system. This model supports academic and personal growth, fostering a generation of students who are career-ready and equipped to thrive in a globalized and dynamic world.

CHAPTER 13
Global Perspectives: What We Can Learn from Other Countries

"The world is a book and those who do not travel read only one page." ~ St. Augustine

The world is vast, and each country's approach to education is shaped by its culture, economy, and values. However, as global challenges become more interconnected, there is a growing realization that education systems must evolve to prepare students for a future that transcends national borders. In the School of Tomorrow, global perspectives are critical, and learning from the experiences of innovative nations is essential for shaping a more adaptable, dynamic, and inclusive education system (Schleicher, 2018).

This chapter explores how countries like Finland, Singapore, Estonia, Germany, and New Zealand have transformed their education systems through innovation, collaboration, and flexibility—and what the School of Tomorrow can learn from these global models. By integrating global best practices, we can create schools that meet our students' needs today and anticipate the demands of a rapidly changing world (Sahlberg, 2015).

Finland: Trust, Flexibility, and Student-Centered Learning

Finland's educational success is rooted in its trust-based system, where teachers are highly trained and given autonomy to adapt their teaching methods to their students' needs. Finnish teachers typically hold master's degrees, and their professional status is similar to that of doctors or lawyers. This trust in teachers translates to less bureaucracy and more freedom to create student-centered classrooms. Instead of standardized tests, Finnish students are evaluated through formative assessments, which inform teaching and learning rather than simply measure outcomes (Sahlberg, 2015).

The Finnish education model is widely documented as one of the best, consistently topping the Programme for International Student Assessment (PISA) rankings. One of Finland's key innovations is its focus on equity; regardless of background, every child can access high-quality education. Finnish schools are also famous for emphasizing well-being, as students have shorter school days, more recess, and a balanced curriculum that includes arts, crafts, and physical education (Schleicher, 2018).

Finland's approach to education is built on the belief that learning should be a joyful and stress-free experience. There is minimal homework, and students are given plenty of time for play and exploration. This reflects Finland's belief that well-being is just as important as academic achievement, a philosophy that the School of Tomorrow embraces fully. By prioritizing the whole child—academic, social, and emotional—schools can create environments where students thrive inside and outside the classroom (OECD, 2022).

Singapore: Rigor, Problem-Solving, and Collaboration

Singapore's education system is globally acclaimed for its rigor and focus on problem-solving, emphasizing logical reasoning, collaboration, and innovation across all subjects. From primary school onward, students engage with a curriculum integrating STEM (science, technology, engineering, and mathematics) with critical thinking, ensuring that even technical subjects encourage creativity and strategic thinking (Schleicher, 2018).

Singapore invests significantly in teacher development through the Academy of Singapore Teachers to support this ambitious curriculum. This academy is a rigorous training ground where educators must complete intensive coursework and hands-on practice before being fully certified. Teachers participate in programs that deepen their content knowledge, instructional techniques, and assessment strategies. This training includes mastery in areas such as differentiated instruction, advanced pedagogical methods, and strategies for fostering critical and creative thinking in students. The academy also emphasizes reflective practice, requiring teachers to continually analyze and improve their teaching methods.

This rigorous training prepares teachers to meet the high expectations of Singapore's educational standards. By equipping them with a strong foundation in pedagogy and a commitment to continuous improvement, Singapore ensures that its educators can effectively guide students through complex, multi-disciplinary subjects, empowering them with skills essential for success in a rapidly changing world (OECD, 2022). This focus on quality teaching underscores the country's belief that exceptional teachers are the backbone of student achievement and a critical component of national progress.

This system fosters student collaboration and encourages active participation, with students frequently working in teams to solve real-world problems. Singapore's Thinking Schools, Learning Nation initiative illustrates the country's commitment to cultivating a nation of learners adept at thinking critically and working collaboratively to solve pressing challenges (OECD, 2022).

In addition to its academic rigor, Singapore's education system emphasizes the importance of continuous improvement. Teachers undergo extensive professional development and are encouraged to engage in lifelong learning to stay current with the latest teaching methods and technologies. This commitment to teacher growth mirrors the Master Teacher and Apprentice Model in the School of Tomorrow, where educators are seen as lifelong learners and mentors (Sahlberg, 2015).

Germany: The Dual-Education System

Germany's dual-education system integrates academic education with vocational training, ensuring students are well-prepared for professional and academic pathways. Students split their time between classroom learning and apprenticeships, often with local businesses or companies. This system allows students to apply theoretical knowledge in real-world settings and develop hands-on skills directly relevant to the job market (OECD, 2022).

In Germany, over 50% of students participate in the dual system, effectively reducing youth unemployment. Companies participating in the system see it as an investment in their future workforce. The success of the dual system highlights the importance of partnerships between schools and industries in preparing students for employment while still in school (Schleicher, 2018).

The School of Tomorrow can learn much from Germany's dual system, particularly in creating career pathways that allow students to gain practical experience while still in school. By partnering with industries and providing students with internships, apprenticeships, and job shadowing opportunities, schools can ensure that students leave with the skills and confidence needed to succeed in the workforce (Sahlberg, 2015).

Estonia: Digital Literacy and Lifelong Learning

Estonia has become a global leader in digital education by prioritizing digital literacy at every level of schooling. Known for its e-Estonia initiative, Estonia integrates technology into every aspect of learning, ensuring that students are familiar with technology and proficient in its use for learning, communication, and innovation (Schleicher, 2018). Estonian schools emphasize coding, robotics, and digital safety in their curricula. Estonia's digital learning platforms, like eKool and Stuudium, also allow teachers, students, and parents to track progress and access resources in real-time.

What makes Estonia unique is its commitment to lifelong learning. Adults are encouraged to continue their education through online courses and professional development opportunities, which are accessible through the same platforms used by younger students. Estonia's success in promoting digital literacy reflects a national commitment to keeping pace with technological advancements and ensuring that citizens of all ages are equipped for a digital future (OECD, 2022).

New Zealand: Experiential Learning and Outdoor Education

In New Zealand, education goes beyond the classroom. The country is known for its emphasis on experiential learning and outdoor education, where students learn by doing and are encouraged to connect with nature and the environment. New Zealand's curriculum promotes critical thinking, creativity, and real-world problem-solving (Sahlberg, 2015).

Students regularly engage in field trips, service learning, and community projects that allow them to apply their knowledge meaningfully. For example, students might participate in a project to restore a local ecosystem, design a sustainable community garden, or work on solutions to address climate change. These experiences help students develop a deep connection to their environment and community while building practical skills (Schleicher, 2018).

New Zealand's emphasis on outdoor learning is also reflected in its physical education and well-being programs, which prioritize student health and emotional well-being. This holistic approach to education aligns with the School of Tomorrow's commitment to educating the whole child—mind, body, and spirit (OECD, 2022).

What We Can Learn: Global Inspiration for Local Innovation

The global education systems highlighted in this chapter offer valuable lessons for creating the School of Tomorrow. These systems share common themes: flexibility, collaboration, innovation, and a commitment to student well-being. By integrating these principles, we can build an education system that prepares students for the challenges and opportunities of the 21st century, where learning is dynamic, equitable, and adaptable to the needs of a globalized world (Schleicher, 2018).

Whether through Finland's trust-based education, Singapore's focus on problem-solving, Germany's dual system, Estonia's embrace of digital literacy, or New Zealand's emphasis on experiential learning, the School of Tomorrow can draw on these international examples to create a future-ready education system that empowers students and supports lifelong learning (Sahlberg, 2015).

The future of education is global, and the lessons learned from innovative education systems around the world can inspire us to create a better, brighter future for all learners (OECD, 2022).

BIBLIOGRAPHY

1. Barnett, W. S., Jung, K., Yarosz, D. J., Thomas, J., Hornbeck, A., Stechuk, R., & Burns, S. (2008). Educational Effects of the Tools of the Mind Curriculum: A Randomized Trial. Early Childhood Research Quarterly, 23(3), 299–313.
2. Buck Institute for Education. (2020). Project-Based Learning Handbook. Retrieved from https://www.pblworks.org.
3. Carnevale, A. P., Smith, N., & Strohl, J. (2013). Recovery: Job Growth and Education Requirements Through 2020. Georgetown University Center on Education and the Workforce.
4. Cubberley, E. P. (1920). The History of Education. Houghton Mifflin Company.
5. Darling-Hammond, L., & Rothman, R. (2011). Teacher and Leader Effectiveness in High-Performing Education Systems. Alliance for Excellent Education and Stanford Center for Opportunity Policy in Education.
6. Education Next. (2018). Cronyism and Its Consequences in Public Education. Retrieved from https://www.educationnext.org.
7. Epstein, J. L. (2018). School, Family, and Community Partnerships: Your Handbook for Action. Corwin Press.
8. Federal Ministry of Education and Research. (2022). Germany's Dual Education System. Retrieved from https://www.bmbf.de.
9. Georgia Department of Education. (2022). Move on When Ready Program. Retrieved from https://www.gadoe.org.
10. Kuypers, L. (2011). The Zones of Regulation: A Curriculum Designed to Foster Self-Regulation and Emotional Control. Social Thinking Publishing.
11. Mann, H. (1848). Annual Reports of the Secretary of the Board of Education of Massachusetts. Massachusetts Board of Education.
12. Mapp, K. L., & Kuttner, P. J. (2013). Partners in Education: A Dual Capacity-Building Framework for Family-School Partnerships. SEDL and U.S. Department of Education.
13. Means, B., & Murphy, R. (2014). The Effectiveness of Online and Blended Learning: A Meta-Analysis of the Empirical Literature. Teachers College Record, 115(3), 1-47.
14. National PTA. (2019). Family Engagement in Student Success. Retrieved from https://www.pta.org.
15. Oakland Unified School District. (2017). Restorative Justice in

Oakland Schools: Implementation and Impact. Retrieved from https://www.ousd.org.
16. OECD. (2018). The Future of Education and Skills: Education 2030. Paris: OECD Publishing.
17. OECD. (2022). Education at a Glance 2022: OECD Indicators. Paris: OECD Publishing.
18. RAND Corporation. (2022). American Teacher Panel Survey Results. Retrieved from https://www.rand.org.
19. Sahlberg, P. (2015). Finnish Lessons 2.0: What Can the World Learn from Educational Change in Finland? Teachers College Press.
20. Schleicher, A. (2018). World Class: How to Build a 21st-Century School System. OECD Publishing.
21. Swiss Federal Statistical Office. (2022). Vocational Education and Training (VET) Statistics. Retrieved from https://www.bfs.admin.ch.
22. Tennessee Department of Education. (2022). Pathways to Prosperity Program. Retrieved from https://www.tn.gov/education.
23. Wallace Foundation. (2021). The Principal as Leader: An Overview of Research on School Leadership. Retrieved from https://www.wallacefoundation.org.

DR. DOUGLAS HENDRIX SR. is a seasoned educational leader with over 20 years of experience driving academic and operational excellence in public schools. Currently serving as the Senior Deputy Superintendent Chief of Staff for Clayton County Public Schools, Dr. Hendrix is known for his strategic vision and hands-on approach to transforming educational systems. He profoundly understands policy development, human resources, and school operations, leading divisions encompassing thousands of staff and students.

Dr. Hendrix has catalyzed meaningful change throughout his career, including boosting graduation rates, increasing enrollment in advanced courses, and implementing innovative programs to enhance learning experiences. His leadership has been particularly impactful during challenging times, such as navigating budget shortfalls and accreditation issues as the district's Chief Human Resources Officer during the Great Recession.

Dr. Hendrix's expertise spans various domains, from curriculum development to capital projects, community partnerships, and legal services. He has consistently committed to educational equity, ensuring all students have access to high-quality learning opportunities. His strategic planning and professional development efforts have left a lasting mark on Clayton County and beyond.

A passionate advocate for modernizing education, Dr. Hendrix's work is informed by his experience as a teacher, principal, and district administrator. His innovative ideas and dedication to student success continue to shape the future of education, making him a respected voice in the field.

Calamity in Commotion County

Dr. Douglas Hendrix Sr.'s upcoming book offers a captivating and insightful exploration of the challenges and triumphs in public education. Through a series of engaging stories, it brings to life the experiences of educators, students, and community members navigating the complexities of today's school systems. Stay tuned for its release!

www.ingramcontent.com/pod-product-compliance
Lightning Source LLC
Chambersburg PA
CBHW071329130726
47996CB00002B/687